Shortcuts & Practical Ways to Survive Marriage

By

Marshell Shelly Do-Bo Johnson

Contents

About the Author 5

Dedication 8

Chapter 1 10

Communication Is Not Easy 10

Chapter 2 22

Uncontrollable Emotions 22

Chapter 3 29

Ego Stroking 29

Chapter 4 40

They Are So Simple; We Make It Hard 40

Chapter 5 50

Time Heals All Wounds 50

Chapter 6 63

Don't Lose No Sleep 63

Chapter 7 79

Shut Up 79

Chapter 8 96

What He Expects From His Wife 96

Chapter 9 113

The Season of Falling Out of Love 113

Chapter 10 128

Pray For His Body, Mind, and Soul 128

Chapter 11 143

Attract and Extract His Gifts and Talents 143

Chapter 12 156

Forgiving Him for Cheating Can Be a Challenge . 156

Chapter 13 167

Learn How to Celebrate Yourself, By Yourself.... 167

Chapter 14 182

He's Not Ready Yet! But Transformation Will Come 182

Chapter 15 200

You Made It To Victory Street! 200

About the Author

My name is Marshell "Shelly Do-Bo" Johnson. I was born in Springfield, Missouri, as the youngest of twelve siblings. As the admittedly spoiled baby of the family, I endured an atypical youth. At the age of seven, I was diagnosed with pectus excavatum, otherwise known as funnel chest, and underwent major surgery, after which I fell into a coma for three weeks and subsequently was sick for several years. This resulted in me missing school and starting my education two years behind other children. I experienced serious educational setbacks and struggled to overcome several learning disabilities in school. However, I persevered, and I was eventually offered a full scholarship in grade to perform as an opera singer. I excelled in the annual state competition and consistently earned the highest ratings. In the middle of ninth grade, I moved to Dallas, Texas, where I overcame the myriad challenges I faced in order to graduate on schedule. I'm a proud mother of two beautiful daughters, and I've been learning in my marriage for 34 years. My husband is gifted, humorous, energetic, and a supportive father to our girls and proud grandfather of our grandson, Austin.

Although I'm extremely grateful for my family, I thought for many years that relocating to Dallas had been a mistake. However, after 36 years in this city, I have realized that this was God's plan all along! I am truly walking by faith, not by sight.

You're probably wondering, "What does this have to do with surviving marriages?" Well, in order to survive in your marriage, you must learn to thrive in all areas of life. For example, in 2009, I lost my sister to breast cancer; in 2014, I lost my first grandson to a lung disease; in 2015, I lost my mother to bone cancer; and in 2017, as I was finally regaining my emotional strength, I was diagnosed with stage 1 breast cancer – though luckily, I was cured later that year!

Although I can only draw upon my life experiences, I have taken my pain and repurposed it into a message of encouragement for other married women through the writing of this book. I am excited to share my journey through marriage with other women seeking advice. Instead of becoming frustrated with your relationship, study this guide to learn how to deal with common marital issues. Marriage is not always easy. It can be complicated, tense, full of anger and resentment, but it can also be the most rewarding adventure you will ever take. If you follow this guide and apply these tactics to your own marriage, the rewards are well worth it.

Dedication

This book is dedicated to my mother Katherine Piggee Bedell, the love that she had for reading books and she's a rose

Special thanks to my husband for the genuine love and support he shows his family on a daily basis. He works extremely hard to give us the best things life has to offer.

Special Thank You;
To my Husband Zebedee Johnson. Two daughters Cerise Reese and Zebretta Johnson, grandson Austin Blake Reese.

Editor – Sonali's Gattani

Co-editor – Shannon Sample

Sample Photos by Schooling Talent & Shane Vanity Beauty

Art Visionaries – Milia Lark & Ernie Bedell Sr.

To all my family and friends.

Chapter 1

Communication Is Not Easy

When I first laid eyes on my husband thirty years ago, I was living with my brother, sister-in-law, and three of my wonderful nieces. We had moved across the town. As we turned the corner toward their new home, I saw a strikingly handsome man sitting alone atop a dark brown Mark IV Lincoln Continental.

He was smoking a cigarette, with a sexy red bandanna wrapped tightly around his forehead. His muscles stretched out a tight, white, fitted sleeveless shirt, and legs toned from years on the football field peeked out from his polyester red shorts. Thirty years later, I can still remember every detail. When I saw him that day, a fire was ignited within me, not due to his physicality but because I felt like I already knew him.

Two weeks later, I spotted him riding his bike down our street, past our house. It was after midnight and once again, he was alone. My anxiety was off the charts as I sprinted toward my bedroom to throw on a brown t-shirt with red, white, and blue shorts. I slid into my flip flops, not bothering to remove the pink sponge rollers in my hair because I did not want to lose my opportunity to meet this man who had been running through my dreams since I first saw him. We ran into each other periodically after that: at the corner store, at the arcade, or simply walking down the street. And every time, he was alone.

The first ninety days after meeting someone reveals a lot about that person's character. For instance, I discovered that my then-crush was intensely private, and I noticed the unique way his body language exposed his need to maintain focus on a singular goal. Simply stated, his drive turned me on!

Shortly afterward, we finally started dating, and I quickly realized we were not communicating with each other. Every issue, every problem, was swept under the rug; when we finally did speak to each other about things that were bothering us, we would simply go in circles. Our lack of communication turned into a nightmare. He thought I was being rude when I interrupted him during arguments, while I thought I was defending myself against untrue personal attacks. We were both too busy justifying our points of view to hear each other's concerns. The most disheartening consequence was that I felt the need to make sacrifices to keep the peace, and those sacrifices came at the expense of everything I loved – such as making music – which only added to my resentment and further hindered our communication.

It took us fifteen years of marriage and some time apart to realize we had a habit of avoiding meaningful communication and to finally seek counseling, but the decision was well worth it. We learned that we were both harboring some form of fear. I can't speak to his fear; that's his story to tell. But I can speak to mine: I was afraid that the multiple setbacks I had experienced with my health, education, and stalled musical aspirations meant my marriage would suffer the same fate; the resulting dissatisfaction was the source of my anger. I had unknowingly given myself a crutch that evolved into a long-term disability by holding onto the past and blaming others for my shortcomings.

We had to put in hard work to resolve our issues, but now we can have calm and rational discussions with one another. Instead of letting my fear convince me that all problems are dire emergencies, I now examine my battles and determine which issues are important enough to make a fuss about. I stopped taking on his private issues and allowing him to turn me into a scapegoat for his problems.

Learning to communicate is a difficult process, but resolving miscommunication becomes easier when you stop to understand how men think. Our counselor shared tools for effective conflict resolution, the most important of which I'm sharing with you now.

Men are private people. I have found that they tend to communicate using actions rather than words, and this extends to the way they display love. Men only share what they want to share, and only when they choose to share it. Women, I know we are more verbal, but we must stop asking so many questions. If your husband doesn't respond to your questions, he simply does not want to answer, and repeating yourself will only frustrate him.

Instead, be patient. Step back and wait for him to come to you. As women, we often want to fix the things we cannot change, whereas men take time to think things through. I am not saying you shouldn't use your voice or share your opinion, but when a man refuses to answer your questions, nagging him won't bring you answers.

After I express my thoughts, I listen to his reply – and then I let it go. There is no reason to confront him again if he doesn't give you the answer you want to hear. Just remember that you have handled your side of the discussion intelligently and sincerely. Women can be stubborn about wanting things to go our way, but this will only hurt your marriage. As you demonstrate your commitment to open and effective communication, he will reciprocate.

Approaching your husband with positivity is only one step toward opening the lines of communication. You must also learn to think the way he does. You can't magically expect him to see your point of view; you have to meet him in the middle and see issues from his perspective as well. Some men are shy, some are opinionated, and some are controlling or outspoken or demanding. Analyze what type of man your husband is so that you can pray to God for the appropriate direction in assessing the roots of your husband's concerns.

For example, say your spouse is upset you have spent too much money on shopping because he believes you have exceeded the household budget, but you insist you used money from your account, so you don't see the problem. If he is a demanding man, he will scream at you regardless of how you respond, but if he is a shy man, then he may simply give you the cold shoulder. Defusing this conflict requires different approaches in both cases.

To communicate with a demanding man, you must understand that he is arguing with you because he feels out of control, and that makes him anxious. When he wants to regain control, his capacity for listening is completely shut down; instead, he wants you to respect what he has said. In this situation, you should pray for insight into why he insists on having things his way and how best to initiate the conversation.

A shy man, on the other hand, maybe unwilling to address the issue first. He does not want to rock the boat or admit there is a problem. To communicate with him, you must take charge and open the conversation yourself. This way, you will show him that you trust him and don't blame him for the breakdown in communication.

But the root of the issue for both types of men is pride. A man's pride can be damaged when he is forced to admit he has made a mistake or misstep. If your husband doesn't see that his pride is negatively impacting your relationship, remaining in the marriage can be difficult, as he may refuse to work with you to open the lines of communication and take initiative when future conflicts arise. However, if in actuality *you* are the one being stubborn and refusing to listen, you must stop and focus on the common goal of achieving peace! As my mama would say, "You don't need two idiots in the argument." Someone must bring peace to the table.

Just as we go to work and resolve the challenges we encounter, so we must approach our relationships with the willingness to chip away at our uncertainties until we find solutions. Yes, it's a lot of work, but it is worth it! Marriage takes work in all areas, from taking out the trash to making sure his credit is in good standing. When men unknowingly carry childhood wounds into adulthood, they bring a wounded spirit into their relationships. But this is who you fell in love with. Remember that there is a great man deep inside him who is striving to get out and love you as you have never known love before. None of us are perfect. We must remain teachable in every aspect of our marriage so that we can learn the value of life and love.

Finally, a note of caution, ladies! When embarking on your journey to improve your communication, be careful who you share your marital concerns with. Not everyone has a forgiving heart or an open mind. Be wary of friends who would try to lead you astray or share your business with others. As long as you aren't experiencing violence or abuse, your friends should support you in the decision to fight for your marriage by espousing acceptance and growth. Assess your friends before taking their advice.

Consider their experience with relationships; question how long they have been with their partners and if they have been married in the past. Examine their attitude when they disagree with someone. Not only will you feel secure that you are receiving genuine advice, but your husband will appreciate you more if you surround yourself with strong, loving women who do not point fingers or hold grudges.

Many marriages end because of a lack of communication or a lack of willingness to fight for improvement. Don't let your relationship go down that road! Do your best to approach communication with an open mind and heart, and feed him with positive energy until he is ready to return the same respect to you.

Here is the road map to improving your communication:

1. Know when to speak, and understand there is strength in silence.

2. Approach disagreements calmly and patiently.

3. Seek God's guidance in working things out together.

4. Enter conversations with a positive attitude.

5. The controversy is a part of growth, so expect it, but handle it with grace.

Chapter 2

Uncontrollable Emotions

Bright and early each morning, before my husband leaves for a long day of work, we share a kiss and tell each other to have a great day. This ritual initially began as a way to express our desire for one another, but over time it has evolved into a comfortable way to start our day and to stay emotionally engaged even when we are no longer in one another's presence. It hasn't always been this way. My husband and I had to overcome several obstacles early in our marriage. Our primary roadblock was learning not to let stress from external circumstances invade our marriage and our home.

If your spouse finds it difficult to let go of stress, he can become abrasive and easily irritable. He may be unable – or unwilling – to allow you to counter his irritation with positivity and help him shake off his negative feelings. Stress (whether external or internal) can easily creep in, and you may find yourself unexpectedly greeted by his uncontrollable emotions. Although his emotions may cause you to feel irrationally upset, you must not let your own emotions spiral out of control. This is the time to be cautious of the words you speak and the tone in which you deliver them. Keep in mind that "uncontrollable emotions" work both ways, and you won't be helping him by allowing your own emotions to grow out of hand.

The irrationality of his emotions could be compounded if he has unresolved issues stemming from having weak relationships with his parents or children, or if he simply has an unforgiving heart. If a man has not been freed from deep-rooted childhood pain and trauma, he will hold his anger close to his heart, unable to find happiness with his current lot in life. The frustration and anger that have anchored themselves deep within his soul will continue to turn him into an unhappy or angry man.

When a man is struggling with his emotions, it is easy to feel like you should throw in the towel and leave him to deal with them on his own. However, although we cannot solve his problems for him, we can acknowledge his past pains, and we can help him work through his anger and aggressive mood swings. It is not easy to help someone who is struggling with anger, but there are ways to help them help themselves.

Determine where your husband's happy places are by noticing where he seems to be more joyful, where he seems to smile more, and where he seems more at peace. My husband is happy when he is relaxing outside around flowers and trees or gazing up into the sky with one foot placed on the back of his truck. He comes from a family that loves gathering beneath the stars, listening to good music, and laughing together as the children play nearby. I noticed that whenever we would invite our family and friends for a barbecue, my husband would wear a huge grin, and when the music came on, it was his time to jam!

Then observe his friends. Do they lift him? How do they treat their wives, and how do they treat you? Does your husband show you love and affection around his friends? His friends may be exacerbating his anger by encouraging him to stew in his emotions instead of finding solutions. Conversely, they may provide a sense of calm for his anger and frustration, and you may be able to encourage him to heal by spending more time around them.

Once you have figured out what his happy places are, you can share yours with him as well. Though they may not perfectly align, the areas that bring you both joy can serve as a starting point for finding mutual methods for decompressing. Whatever your husband's chosen method, he will eventually start to relax. The stress that he has been carrying will vanish and will hopefully be replaced by laughter and good humor.

To be imperative. You must keep the ball in your husband's court. He has to see that he is fighting his own battles and that he must fight for himself. Remember that men are very private creatures. Let him vent if he needs to let off some steam, or leave him alone if he doesn't want to be bothered. If he starts to pick a fight with you, do not participate. Eventually, he will become tired of fighting himself.

That said, if he responds dismissively every day, then it is time to talk about what is worrying him and why his emotions are taking control of his mind so frequently. You may find it best for you to step out of his view for a few hours, let him relax, and approach him with a listening ear and an open mind once he's had a chance to calm down.

Remind him that you love him and want to help him. Remind him of how you have helped each other in the past, and how sharing your troubles has yielded positive results before. Don't give up if he doesn't immediately respond to you; he will eventually realize that he can be open and vulnerable with you.

Here is the road map to responding to your husband's uncontrollable emotions:

1. Speak positively and avoid overtly negative conversations.
2. Take the time to share your happy places together.

3. Inform him of the way his actions and anger make you feel.

4. Excuse yourself from his presence when his emotions are out of control.

Chapter 3

Ego Stroking

Do you know any man that doesn't like to be praised? Some men do extra just to receive praise from their wives or partner. Many men love showing off their knowledge about home repairs, diagnosing car problems, building furniture – they like to prove that they know what to do. It's a man's way of showing his wife that he is the only person who can make her happy and that he is capable of handling any issues that come her way.

When I first married my husband, I didn't give him enough praise or show him enough appreciation. I didn't know that I should tell my husband the yard looked great or thank him for washing my car.

When he cooked delicious meals, I didn't understand that I should complement him and ask him to cook for me again soon.

It took me a while to learn that ego-stroking plays a very important role in marriage! We all want to receive praise and validation from the person we love, and when we don't, our dissatisfaction can drive a wedge into the relationship. However, while women are strong and comfortable with crying and expressing emotions, men lash out and get angry or blame other people. Many men did not receive much appreciation when they were young; as a result, they didn't learn how to ask for acknowledgment or how to return praise to others.

Ladies, it falls to us to fill that blank space in our husbands' hearts by stroking their egos and reminding them they have value. Men's values and standards must be acknowledged; stroking their ego and pride motivates them to keep doing whatever gained them appreciation. We must pour as much love as we can into our husbands to help them learn how to release their stress, employ compassion, and swallow their pride. If we can manage this, we can nip numerous issues in the bud.

Even if you don't see an immediate reaction from your husband, know that he is receiving and accepting every gesture of your love. Don't lose heart! You are a healer, here to build up his self-esteem. By stroking his ego, you will inspire him to become a new and kinder man. If you stop lifting him, you will quickly find out how important your support is to him. A few words of praise can affect his whole attitude!

Whatever your husband's strengths are, give him ample opportunities to use them. When he tries to showcase his knowledge and skills, support him, and demonstrate respect for his time and efforts. Doing so will teach him to respect your feelings as well; once he learns what is important to you, he will keep those things in mind.

For instance, my husband is a mechanic, so I make sure that he is the first person I ask to look at my car when it is having issues. All I have to say is, "Baby, I'm hearing a strange noise coming from my car," and he'll have it taken care of in a jiffy! He likes being asked before I take my car to a mechanic because it makes him feel as though I value his opinion above the opinions of others. If your spouse is not mechanically inclined, you can let him decide where to take your car for repairs, as having control over this will let him feel knowledgeable in his specific way.

My husband also enjoys doing yard work. He loves when his yard looks green and healthy, and he loves it, even more, when I cook a nice meal for him and compliment him on his perfect landscaping. Yardwork is not a hobby I enjoy, but I make sure to tell my husband how much I appreciate the effort he puts into beautifying our yard. When I ask if I can bring him a cup of cold water, or when I check on how he is faring in the blistering hot sun, he feels acknowledged and validated.

Expressing appreciation for your husband's talents is a wonderful way to show your love, but you can take things to the next level by joining him. When I help my husband plant flowers, it deepens our sense of connection, which in turn brings us both joy. Supporting his talents and gifts is the key to touching his heart. When you compliment your husband, he will feel that his work has been recognized. Giving him the attention he craves can be as simple as asking questions about his to-do list from time to time, as even this small gesture informs him that you are watching him and care about his projects.

Don't forget to stroke your husband's ego in front of his family and friends! Rave about his barbecue, or brag about the entertainment center he built when your friends come to visit. Outwardly expressing your appreciation for your spouse will not only inspire him but can also positively influence other couples, who will see your loving interactions and may try to replicate them in their relationships. If your husband frequently cooks for you, tell him that he has to make this dish the next time you host a party. It makes a man feel good when his wife has his back and brags about his accomplishments. I'm not saying you must constantly shower your spouse with affection, but it is an awesome feeling when that expression becomes a natural expression from you.

Ego stroking can be difficult, particularly if you think your husband should stroke your ego before you stroke his. However, the more positive your approach to him is, the faster he will return that positivity to you. As I've said before, a positive attitude helps maintain peace in your relationship. There are many things we cannot change; we can only do our part and wait for change to come.

What has worked for my marriage has been unyielding faith and prayer. Two scriptures that I rely on are Romans 12:2 – "And be not conformed to this world: but be ye transformed by the renewing of your mind, that ye may prove what is that good, and acceptable, and perfect, will of God" – and Proverbs 18:22 – "Whoso findeth a wife findeth a good thing, and obtaineth favor of the Lord." These scriptures remind me that I have been utterly chosen, prepared, and equipped to handle all that He expects from me – including how to best support my husband.

Hold onto what you know this man is worth because your support and belief in him will help him mature. Men are well aware of what they are looking for in their partners, and ego-stroking is definitely included on their lists of expectations!

Another crucial aspect of maintaining your relationship is being aware of timing. When you give a piece of advice to a man or constructive criticism, he may think you are trying to control him, causing him to rebel if he doesn't like being controlled. To preempt this conflict, phrase your words with intent and kindness so you don't sound threatening. Also, don't praise him excessively, as this will cause your words to lose their meaning. Instead, be mindful of when he is feeling upset or insecure. If he appears to be struggling, build him back up by focusing on his strengths and giving him perspective on recovering from downfalls. This will take time, prayer, and wisdom. Successful ego-stroking is dependent on using appropriate timing; it takes patience to rebuild a man whose soul has been damaged.

The struggle seems to be intensified for millennials. In this current day and age, there are myriad distractions and external stressors such as social media that make it difficult to maintain healthy relationships and recover from setbacks. Additionally, it is an unfortunate fact that many members of generation Y have experienced being raised in two homes rather than in a single, two-parent home. Many younger adults have not witnessed their parents lovingly working through conflict, so they do not know how to handle differences of opinion, let alone how to encourage and build up their mates.

Even when you feel tired, try to muster the energy to share some kind words with your husband. The smallest compliment can make him feel like the king of the world, and the effects of your ego-stroking will add up in the end. When he doesn't have to tell you what to do or what he wants from you, he will appreciate you even more, and you will see positive outcomes. Your husband knew exactly what he was looking for when he met you, and he knows you are capable of meeting his expectations. You have to remind him that you love him, that you notice when he runs you a bath or when he changes the oil in your car.

Of course, it is important to balance praising your husband with keeping him humble. Don't be afraid to point out his flaws – in a loving way, of course. After all, a healthy relationship will encourage you both to grow. Men often forget that we have expectations of them just as they have expectations of us, so a gentle reminder from time to time will hold him accountable. Receiving compliments from the one he loves will give him a natural high, and he will be more inclined to listen to the points you raise.

Here is the road map to successful ego-stroking:

1. Focus on his strengths

2. Rebuild him when he experiences downfalls.

3. Meditate on scripture

4. Praise him frequently and sincerely.

Chapter 4

They Are So Simple; We Make It Hard

When you were a little girl, did you ever go to the fair with your family? Did you find yourself enchanted by the colorful rides and loud music and delicious food, the rows and rows of tents lined with prizes big and small? I went to the local fair every year with the same goal: to win the great big teddy bear hanging high above the ring toss. Something about the stuffed toy – maybe its soft fur, maybe its huggable size – exuded a feeling of security and protection that I desperately craved.

Our husbands expect the same love from us that we gave to our teddy bears as kids. Back then, I found comfort in being engulfed in my oversized bear's arms, where nothing could penetrate that protective barrier and hurt me. As simple as that may seem, I imagine our partners want us to show them that same trust and excitement every chance we get.

Simplicity is the key to a successful relationship. Many situations have simple solutions, but we needlessly complicate them with our need to maintain control. Instead, keep things simple by learning to let them go. Although it feels good to receive validation of your perspective, it becomes easy to chase after that validation at the expense of your relationship's stability. There is no doubt, that having your viewpoint challenged feels unpleasant, but rather than feeling offended and pushing back, there are times when surrendering may be best.

Make a habit of occasionally checking the pulse of your relationship. Check-in with your spouse periodically to understand what is going on in his life and what is on his mind. You can learn a lot by simply sitting back and observing his actions. When you are ready to make your observations known, approach him with patience, and ask to speak with him at his convenience. Taking the time to recalibrate and refocus will help you avoid unnecessary arguments.

Planning.

Do you ever find yourself trying to talk to your husband about something only for him to tell you he's busy? Or maybe he has plans that conflict with your schedule, but he is unwilling to change them for you. It's easy to feel frustrated in these situations and lash out at him. However, if it upsets you when your spouse doesn't change his plans for you, you are making things difficult for yourself by being selfish.

Instead of forcing your husband to accommodate you, ask him when his schedule is open and wait until then to talk with him. In the meantime, look at the situation from different perspectives and consider what compromise or solutions you can offer to keep the peace; that is how to keep things simple. He will appreciate your independence and initiative, and if you are patient with him, he will work with you to change his schedule without having to be asked again.

Of course, sometimes you simply have to accept that his schedule doesn't align with yours and that you will have to push back your plans. He doesn't always like the same activities you do, just as you don't share the same interests he does. (Even after 31 years of marriage, I still can't understand my husband's love for car shows and action movies!) At these times, even though you may feel offended, don't complicate things by nagging him to cancel his plans to accompany you. Accept his decision with grace and positivity.

Most importantly, ensure your schedule is realistic and accommodates both of you. For example, my husband prefers to plan out his projects before starting them because he can become overwhelmed when he is faced with unexpected obstacles. It took me several years to understand that he won't do things the moment I ask him to because he has to think about what I requested and how he can add them to his agenda. Now, I simply tell him what needs to be done and let him choose his priorities.

If you find yourself burning with anger because he isn't doing things your way, take some time off and enjoy yourself – take up a hobby, work out, join a book club, or a meetup group. When you're surrounded by people who share your mindset and interests, you will be motivated to remain positive.

Not to mention, your husband will appreciate you indulging in positive activities to enhance your life.

Finances.

Strong finances and financial literacy are important in marriage, as financial strength is a sign of stability. If your husband is knowledgeable in this area, then you are on the right track. He will have no problem showing you how to manage your spending habits and balance you're spending against the household budget.

However, if your husband does not know how to handle money, gently suggest handling the finances together or allowing you to take the lead. Keep it simple! Rather than assuming he will learn to manage his finances on his own, pull his credit report and bank statements, and show him exactly where his money is going. Stop supporting his bad habits! When you're married, his poor finances affect *both* of you.

Likewise, if he asks you to make some sacrifices to save up for your household bills or your next large purchase, trust him, and work with him to find a solution that keeps you both happy. Be honest about how long you are willing to cut back on your spending, and see how you can contribute financially to show that you care about the household finances, too. Just don't let your arguments spiral out of control. Arguments over money can be like a virus, creeping into your marriage and causing it to deteriorate before you know what has happened. Make every effort to respect the agreement you made, and when you find yourself arguing, step away to calm down.

More importantly, don't let money outshine your love for each other. Remember that you are a team; you are partners. You should be approaching this issue together rather than imposing your individual desires and expectations onto each other. Strive for positivity at all times, even in the middle of disagreements, and misunderstandings. If you show your husband that you can choose your battles wisely and handle your emotions maturely, he will follow your example. Managing your finances can be simple; there's no need to make it as complicated as we sometimes do.

Housekeeping.

When I was younger, my mother always said to me, "Cleanliness is next to godliness." Maybe your job keeps you busy, or you find cleaning and housekeeping mundane. However, that's no excuse to let your house fall into disrepair! You have many options for keeping the house clean. Research maid services in your area if you have the budget for it, or talk to your husband about splitting the chores.

Housekeeping can become the source of the biggest arguments between you and your husband, especially if one of you is very organized and the other isn't. But you cannot live in a dirty house, so you should compromise! Sit down with your husband and evaluate how you each contribute to keeping your house clean. Agree regarding what chores each of you are responsible for, and hold each other accountable.

I'll admit, achieving change can be difficult, especially if your husband isn't on board. If he rebels against you, only God can change his heart. Until then, stay patient, and let him grow. Take responsibility for your role in maintaining a peaceful atmosphere in your home, and seek God's wisdom to keep your marriage strong. It is easy enough to say "for better or for worse" at the altar on your wedding day, but upholding that vow can be challenging at times. Learn to balance work with play, and enjoy each other's company.

If you keep your word and take care of your responsibilities, he will give you the same teddy bear love you've given him and enfold you in his arms with a promise to keep you safe.

Here is the road map to keeping it simple:
1. Learn how to simplify your life.
2. Work toward financial stability.
3. Don't let fear stop your growth.
4. Make plans together.
5. Take care of yourself and your home.

Chapter 5

Time Heals All Wounds

People ask me what the worst years of my marriage were, how long it took me to realize I was hurting, and how long it took to see a change. Let me start by stating this: The day that you say "I do," emotional conflicts start to infiltrate your marriage. Do you remember being a kid and spinning 'round and 'round in circles until you were dizzy? Marriage is the same. The day that you agree to be his wife, you have to open your eyes and turn on your listening ears. At first, you will feel the euphoria of spinning at high speeds, but as you grow together, you will face countless challenges that threaten the strength of your relationship and leave you dizzy.

When you wanted to stop spinning like a child, you didn't come to an immediate standstill; you slowed down gradually to avoid throwing up. Approach these challenges with a similar mindset: slowly, patiently, but persistently. Sometimes those challenges will be easy to overcome, and other times, you might feel like you'll never stop spinning, but no matter how long you find yourself spinning, you must hold on tight! All relationships undergo tests, but as long as you don't give up, you will win each battle in time. You will both stumble and grow and learn together until you know each other's priorities and habits. When you learn to respect each other's priorities without complaint, healing begins. Let me share the words that every married couple needs to hear: Time heals all wounds.

Storms visit every relationship, bringing distractions without any warning, like tornadoes – quiet and distant but setting off sirens telling you to take cover. However, weathering these types of storms is a part of strengthening your relationship! Even the strongest storms pass with time; you just have to take cover until then. A lot of women give up on good men too soon because they run for cover at the first sight of trouble. However, weathering a few storms will show you how sturdy your relationship with your partner is. A good man stands through the storms and is willing to rebuild once the storm has passed, whereas men who are simply having fun will not want to deal with the messy aftermath! From the very first date, you should be evaluating how your partner responds to storms brewing on the horizon. Some men are simply having fun and looking for independent women who don't want serious relationships; these types of men may not want commitment.

Just as you stock storm shelters with supplies to make waiting out the tornado easier, you can make the journey towards achieving peace easier by practicing patience and approaching your partner with empathy. Ultimately, however, wisdom comes with time. The mistakes you make are necessary for teaching experiences. Trust that God has your well-being in mind and is sending you these obstacles to make you a stronger woman and a better wife, and ask Him to guide you along the right path. No matter how many storms you face in marriage, don't lose your faith.

When I was going through a stressful time in my marriage, God sent me a mentor who, due to being nineteen years older than me, had much more experience than me and shared her wisdom freely every day. She encouraged me to challenge myself, and she helped me realize I had placed my relationship with God on the back burner in favor of keeping my husband happy. However, this had the unintended consequence of weakening my relationship, as I had no one to turn to for guidance on how to weather the storms I was facing. I needed to nurture my relationship with God again and put Him first in my life, my mentor told me; only then could He guide me in the correct direction and help me mend my floundering relationship.

So I concentrated on asking God to heal me, to help me be a better wife, and to help me focus on Him. At first, my husband didn't understand why I was no longer at his beck and call. He couldn't recognize that I wasn't being fulfilled. As time passed, though, my husband started noticing the changes God instilled in me, and he joined me in following where God was leading me, even if he found some parts of my relationship with God challenging to accept.

Now I am totally obedient to God's guidance. He taught me how to weather even the harshest of storms. He showed me I needed to let go of what I didn't have the power to change. I received understanding and patience from Him that changed my life for the better and healed our marriage. It simply took some time to receive God's plentiful rewards. Eventually, my husband also recognized that God had been proving Himself to us for a while, and now he knows to keep his opinion to himself and go with the flow. He is aware that God is always good and keeps us covered.

My mentor would frequently ask me, "What are you mad about? Is this his issue or yours? What is the true reason for your arguments?" Her words were eye-opening to me. I started analyzing every argument I had with my husband to see whether he was the root of the issue or I was. It was only then that I noticed the frequency with which he pointed out how I was upsetting him without acknowledging how he was upsetting me. Coming to terms with his tendency to blame me for every problem took years, but I finally realized that I couldn't try to win every argument. Only time can heal every pain and disagreement you will have in a relationship.

We're all quick to point fingers, and we all want to give voice to the anger growing in our hearts because it makes us feel heard and helps us convince ourselves that our emotions matter. However, you have to learn not to give that anger an outlet. Your emotions matter whether or not he sees that. If you know his criticism of you is not true, sweep it away, and don't take his words to heart. Adopt a positive mentality, and remember that you don't need to fight his battles for him. If he is a contentious person, that is his struggle.

If you find your arguments spiraling out of control, making you wonder why you ever married him and why you're staying with him instead of finding someone better, know that this pain, too, will heal with time. Surely you've heard people say, "You won't miss him until your well runs dry." Ladies, I'm telling you that's a true statement!

Take couples who reunite after a long time apart as an example. These couples love each other enough to outweigh the bad times, remember the good times, and accept that God's timing is the correct timing. These people were made better and more mature by time – time spent thinking about how they could have dealt with things differently, time spent planning how they would react upon seeing each other again, time spent fanning the flames of love and healing from past mistakes. They knew that they had leaned on each other, cried on each other's shoulders, and forged a bond so strong that even though something had caused them to walk away from each other, they loved each other enough to overcome that rift.

I, myself am proof that time heals all broken hearts eventually. My husband and I experienced separation several times throughout our marriage. Each time, the separation allowed us to think about what was causing our arguments and learn the importance of respecting each other's concerns. With enough time, I remembered why I had married him and came back to him, and our marriage grew stronger, but we needed the time to consider our actions. Ladies, if you find yourselves in times of trouble, ask whether you have given time a chance to heal the conflict you are facing.

When you do return to him after an argument, keep forgiveness in your heart. Forgiveness is a word repeated in every sermon and stated multiple times at the pulpit, but so many of us do not forgive, and we surely don't forget. However, I am telling you, we must forgive to be able to heal from destruction and move forward! The inability to forgive is a disease within the mind that rots the heart. So many women hold anger in their hearts for a long time because they reject forgiveness, which comes only with time, patience, and wisdom from God. These women are too impatient to wait for God to move in His own time.

We have to understand the magnitude of what time can accomplish. Ladies, you cannot change your man, but if his love and commitment to you are true, time will soften his rough edges, and our Heavenly Father will pull forth the changed and improved man hiding within him. He must receive his healing from God, and God's healing must come in its own time.

Married life works like a seesaw: You have to give 100 percent effort at the high points and 200 percent at the low points! The lowest points of the ride are the toughest, and they will stay that way until you find your equilibrium. Balancing the highs and lows takes work and true commitment to each other! In these times, turn to God for guidance and patience; hold on tight, and don't let go of His unchanging hand. As the Bible states, the family that prays together stays together (Proverbs 22:6). Give God all glory and thanks for setting this test, and work with your husband as a team to pass it. When you finally make it off the ground, you will find God raining blessings upon your marriage – not just a drizzle, but a full downpour.

Of course, some prayers take you across the river and through the woods before giving you an answer. This is because change occurs gradually, bit by bit, day by day. Listen closely to your heart to identify what you need to work on correcting. Activate your faith and strengthen your relationship with God because He will reflect that effort back at you! A woman who works to heal her soul and achieve inner peace shines in the dark. Light follows her everywhere she goes. So stand up and fight the good fight to save your marriage. Every relationship involves its fair share of pain and discomfort, but this is no excuse to give up!

I advise every married couple to sit down with an older couple who has been married for more than 50 years and listen to what they have to say about creating long-lasting marriages. You ought to truly pay attention when they describe the ups and downs they went through and the effort they put into staying together when they hated each other's guts. You will see that with time, true love conquers all. Ladies, if he doesn't truly love you, he will make it clear sooner or later, but giving him the time to prove himself is the first step to healing your marriage.

As a piece of advice from the box experience:

"Stay true to yourself and faithful to your marriage, and your growth will never stop."

And when you have a moment, pray to the Lord. Tell Him, "Thank you for allowing me to learn deeply and love sincerely in these difficult times as we work to mend our marriage. I know that our time is not your time, but your time is the right time, and the time by which life flows. Grant us the strength to fight for what is right in your eyes and stand firm in our beliefs." In Jesus' name, amen!

Here is the road map to having faith in time:

1. Pray before you give up on your marriage because healing requires prayer and faith.
2. Focus on achieving inner peace, and watch your external circumstances change.
3. View mistakes as vehicles for self-growth.
4. Don't place blame; just present the answer, and then let your pain go.
5. Trust that time heals all wounds if you give it the opportunity.

Chapter 6

Don't Lose No Sleep

Let me share an unexpected turn in my life. In 2016, I resigned from my job of 14 years to move forward as a music producer and songwriter, a dream I had harbored since childhood. The shift was challenging, but I believed God had much more in store for me to accomplish upon this Earth, and I trusted Him to take my life in the right direction. I strove for success on faith alone.

This decision wasn't easy, though. I tossed and turned at night. I felt I couldn't simply wake up my husband and state I was quitting my job because God had told me to. I already sounded crazy to myself! What would he think? How would I explain that I had been directed to make this radical decision by God? I fought against myself for four months, wondering how to wrap my mind around this walk of faith, even as my family and friends encouraged me to just keep trusting God.

Too much natural, God-given talent gets placed on hold for no reason. So many women place their dreams and passions on the back burner so they can please their men. We worry about what others will think and what our husbands will say, so we say to ourselves, "I'll go back to college next year; I'll try for that job when I get more experience; I'll apply for that new house in two years because I'm not ready for that responsibility right now." We are so afraid of upsetting our husbands that we stay discontent instead.

Well, I'm not saying that you shouldn't be there for your spouse, but a man loves when his wife can pick herself up and find a purpose aside from chasing him down. Our Heavenly Father expects us to acknowledge the gift that has been placed inside each of us, too. If you had set your passion aside to focus on your marriage, it's time to pick it back up! Get back on your grind and don't stop until you have reached your goal. Most importantly, don't lose sleep over nonsense!

Some of us tend to worry about situations we cannot change. We toss and turn at night, imagining all the "*what if*s" and "*could have been*s". We worry about the goals we haven't achieved, and we worry we are running out of time. We try to formulate new plans, and we weigh the pros and cons of every conceivable course of action. Meanwhile, our hair is graying because we haven't been sleeping, and we certainly aren't getting any younger!

Instead, save your energy to worry about things you can change! You should set your mind on positive thoughts so that you can sleep peacefully because

I'm telling you, you deserve your beauty sleep! Before you get into bed, write your goals for the next day in a journal so you have a record of your intentions. Listen to soothing music to wind down. Then tell yourself firmly, "I can't change what other people think about my decisions right now. I'll tackle those problems when I wake up."

Your worries won't magically go away if you follow this routine, but you will remind yourself that some things are out of your control, and it doesn't do anyone any good to worry about that. I still experienced terrible anxiety when I finally faced my husband, even though I was obedient to His word and knew I had to follow His will. However, when God is in it, He transforms the situation from something out of a horror movie to a perfect solution. Placing my trust in God opened myriad doors for both me and my marriage. My husband and I realized what was truly important: our love for each other, our faith, and blessing others with what we had learned. Supporting other couples became our greatest passion; we didn't want them to lose sleep the way we did when I was preparing to make this drastic, God-given change.

Therefore, I am telling you this, ladies: When you have been directed to make a drastic and unexplainable move in your life, that is God moving you toward your dreams! You may not find an easy explanation in your soul, but don't be discouraged. Listen to the small voice that keeps you up at night, telling you what He wants you to do and encouraging you to make that move! One day you will have no choice but to take that step. God delivers answers in strange and inexplicable ways, but you will realize down the line that there could not have been a better outcome.

We lose sleep because we refuse to do what we have been told. But there is no reason to be afraid of change. Our fears are often unfounded, and we use them as excuses. You should not lose sleep fretting over the outcomes of your actions. So long as you keep your husband informed and fulfill your wifely duties, you should not hesitate to chase your dreams!

You may not like leaving your spouse alone for an extended period, but taking a break from each other will only strengthen your marriage. You will develop trust in each other, knowing that even when you stop and smell the roses – when you take a walk by yourself or travel abroad with your friends without him, or when he takes time off to think things through or go fishing with his friends – you will inevitably return to each other's side. This trust will allow you to share the instructions God has given you when you feel you need to make a drastic change.

I can't explain the importance of missing each other when you trust each other 100 percent. The roots of your relationship will thicken and grow stronger, wider, longer. As they say, absence makes the heart grow fonder. The sweetest experience in my marriage was when I realized the roots of our love had burrowed deep into the ground and anchored themselves, meaning it was time to simply enjoy each other's presence and live our lives. I so often think about the sleep I lost throughout my marriage, only to understand years later that trust was all I needed.

If you do not build this trust and instead break away suddenly to chase your particular ambitions, your husband may feel jealous that you have redirected your ardor to another pursuit. He may even worry that you will stop paying attention to him. When a man is fighting insecurities and jealousy, he may feel the need to control you. In these circumstances, you must remember that his insecurities are his problem, not yours. Determine first and foremost what the best course of action is for you because catering to his ego will only hurt you in the end. If he truly loves you, he will be willing to change for the better, and he will make a concerted effort not to get carried away wallowing in self-pity. Do not lose sleep over his insecurities! It is a waste of your time and energy. You should not totally dismiss his feelings, but by standing firm in your decisions, you will show him that he needs to correct his behavior.

It is important to focus on yourself instead of trying to micromanage your husband's emotions. At one point in my marriage, I realized I had spent so long paying attention to his life that I had stopped taking care of myself. I was drained and unhappy. I was unable to accept my situation, and I only saw myself as a victim, a failure who had wasted half her life and far too much money on failed endeavors. I felt unattractive physically and emotionally. Eventually, I was able to regain control over my emotions by asking God for help, but I lost a lot of sleep in the process.

You have to realize that our minds play games with us, telling us we are unattractive and worthless even if we have evidence to the contrary. This, of course, makes us more upset, creating a cycle of negative emotions that feeds on itself. If you stop focusing on yourself, you become vulnerable to this cycle, so you have to learn to release your resentment toward your husband and your anger so you can be honest with yourself! Understand that you must suppress your fear of depression and unhappiness, and believe that life's trials will solve themselves. Your husband will be able to understand the emotions swirling inside you if he is in the right position with God, but if he is not, don't lose any sleep! His burdens are not yours to bear.

When I say to stop fretting over things you can't change, I mean your husband, too! Men are fickle. You can fight to save your relationship for years and years, but your efforts won't make a difference if he decides to stay firm in his actions and behaviors. You need to remember that your husband is just a man. There is no reason to give him absolute power over your actions and emotions.

The bottom line is do not lose sleep over a man! I don't mean to sound cynical, but there is no such thing as a perfect marriage. You will face troubles, you will argue with each other, you will feel unheard and unloved at times. However, know that these arguments are only temporary bumps in the road, and just as when you are driving, you need to approach them calmly, slowly, and with the certainty that you will soon leave them behind you. Getting yourself worked up every time you face conflict will only give you unnecessary grief.

If you feel yourself losing control, be careful not to overcompensate by taking control of your marriage and trying to dominate your husband. You want to strengthen your relationship, not lose it! If you are trying to take control from your husband, you may end up losing sleep over the guilt you feel for stepping out of your role. Stay true to yourself as a wife, and you will welcome comfort and security into your soul. Much like we maintain our balance on the rain-slick pavement by placing our feet carefully and purposefully, you will maintain the balance and security of your relationship by approaching your husband with respect and care.

Remember that your husband doesn't like being smothered. Nor should you let him smother you! Do not lose the vision you have for yourself. Remain confident; don't worry too much about keeping him happy. True happiness needs to lie within you because only then will *"the peace of God, which transcends all understanding…keep your hearts and minds"* (Philippians 4:7). Your focus will be clear to your husband, and once you achieve that level of peace, your husband will hunger for your attention and do everything he can to keep you happy. You cannot focus so intensely on his emotions and reactions that you forget to strengthen your faith.

It is easy to fall prey to tunnel vision – the tendency to focus on a single issue to the exclusion of all else – when you worry to no end about your husband's emotions. However (and this may sound crazy), I believe tunnel vision shows you exactly what you *can't* change in your relationship! Instead of focusing on his turmoil, turn your focus to your own goals; only then will you be able to renew your mind. Stop letting stressful emotions grow in your mind as a result of your husband's actions. Instead, invite God into your soul, that private place where no one else is invited, and ask Him to help you find peace within yourself! You should not be losing sleep because your every thought revolves around your husband. Your role is to elevate and stimulate your husband into being a godly man, not to center your entire life and future on him. Just do your part and nothing more!

Learning about tunnel vision helped me heal. I started meditating every night to seek peace within myself and shift my focus to appropriate goals. Ladies, I highly recommend trying meditation. It reframes how you see yourself and encourages you to think positively and choose your battles properly. Your spiritual growth will amaze you. There is nothing like having a clear vision of who you are. When you reach that goal, please wrap your arms around yourself and keep shining your light!

My mother once said to me, "Shelly, you have a lot to learn. You get mad too quickly about what doesn't matter!" Her words of wisdom have proven true time and time again; we can keep more peace in our marriages than we believe if we simply learn to let the insignificant things go. One of my faults in my relationship was that I often held tight to negative thoughts without any evidence to back up my concerns. I justified my crooked mindset by claiming God has given every woman powerful intuition, but I truly took my concerns overboard, and I almost destroyed my marriage.

However, I remembered my mother's words, and I tried to apply them to my relationship. Ladies, when I focused on seeking peace within myself instead of on negativity, my marriage took a sharp turn toward the light. My wisdom kicked in, and after the first time my husband and I resolved an argument without shouting at each other, my maturity took flight. I said to myself, "Mother, you would be proud of me because I am learning how to accept what I can't change every day."

If you let your spouse become the focal point of your life's journey, you will stop focusing on your calling just to keep him happy. You will hide from your loving friends and drown yourself in sorrow. Before you know it, you will be knee-deep in depression, unable to sleep because you have surrendered your life to him instead of loving yourself. Avoiding this slippery slope is crucial to living a meaningful life. Stay alert, stay confident, and stay true to yourself. Don't hesitate to let him know that you will love him with all your heart, but always strive to better your future simultaneously.

Maya Angelou once stated, "If you don't like something, change it. If you can't change it, change your attitude." Nothing will improve unless you make a concerted effort to improve things. Don't lose sleep over things you can't change. Just work to make things better.

Here is the road map to not losing your sleep:

1. Write down your thoughts and feelings in a journal every night before you go to sleep.
2. Disengage from conflict and indulge in self-care to calm down.

3. Meditate to get a clear understanding of your thoughts and goals.

4. Focus on improving yourself instead of trying to change your husband.

5. Remember that you cannot control every conflict that comes your way; you can only control yourself. Change yourself, and your husband will follow.

Chapter 7

Shut Up

My mother used to tell us all the time to "rest our minds." When I was younger, I didn't know what she meant by that, but her meaning became clear as I got older: You don't have to comment on everything you hear. It is good to speak after you have had a chance to analyze and organize your observations, but you should not speak without thinking twice. When you rashly speak what's on your mind, nine times out of ten, it will come out the wrong way. However, when you stop and think about what you are feeling, you will have time to phrase your comments positively and state your point maturely.

I know many women who are single due to their opinionated views which make men completely disinterested in them. Having strong opinions on everything, insisting that you won't do certain things or take directions from a man, maintaining the comfort of your mindset, and refusing to change – all of these stubborn decisions are dangerous to your relationship. After all, as stated in Proverbs 21:19, "Better to dwell in the wilderness, than with a contentious and angry woman." If you don't dig deep and uproot the stubbornness from the mind, you will have a miserable marriage. Stop to listen to your heart before you speak!

The fact of the matter is that many women need to learn when to shut up. We often feel that in addition to expressing ourselves, we must win every battle, but this isn't true. If you are always trying to get the last word, you'll only end up driving your husband away with your rudeness and disrespect. You won't give him a reason to stick around. Instead, take control of your tongue and learn to monitor the situation.

After thirty-three years of marriage, my husband and I have disagreed on countless issues, but we're still together! I'm telling you, there's no possible way to remain married for so long without achieving growth. The secret shortcut to finding harmony is to monitor your mouth because when he is mad, he's not going to hear what you are saying anyway. When he refuses to share what's on his mind or what's troubling his heart, there's nothing you can do to change his decision. He has to be willing to respond actively. Once again, the theme of "keeping the ball in his court" comes into play. Don't you dare start dribbling the ball down your own court because you'll quickly realize you and he, both are playing two different games! If he isn't mature, he is invariably going to complain about something, no matter how hard you try to assuage his concerns. He must want to release his concerns without any struggles.

However, if you choose to step back and stay quiet, no matter how hard that is for you, the situation will start to turn around. My pastor always said, "If you wrestle with pigs, you'll get dirty, too." What this means is, if you try to match your husband's irritation and focus only on winning the argument, you'll end up frustrating yourself. One of you has to remain peaceful and maintain your composure, shining a light so that darkness won't settle in your home. A relationship that lives in the dark is hard to nurture, and this is the outcome you will face if you let your tongue run loose or display the cold shoulder.

You must be willing to change your mindset. When you are angry, turn that energy toward another activity: renewing your mind. I am not saying you should ignore your feelings, but don't waste your time thinking of ways to get back at your husband. There is nothing to be gained from bringing up past disagreements or stooping down to a petty level. Ladies, we are the light of our homes; never forget that. So stop, pray, and think before you speak. It's only fair. Controversy will rear its ugly head in your marriage more often than you expect, but you have to respond to those situations with a sound mind.

Some women are married to men who hide their emotions. If you are one of these women, keep moving! Sooner or later, the light within you will overtake his negative energy, and the spirit of negativity will have nowhere to go but out the door! He will become more comfortable with his emotions and with being vulnerable, just by being around you. The positive energy you emanate will take full control, and that is when the healing will begin inside of him. It is amazing when a man successfully acquires the radiance of peace and the glow of liveliness, and he will only do so when he is encouraged by the woman he has fallen in love with. We have all heard this phrase: Behind every great man, there is a great woman!

Another place where you should choose your battles is family disputes. Both of you will have issues with your family, but you need to keep those issues separate from your married business. Entangling your family in your marriage conflicts will only damage your marriage. Remember that you don't come from his type of familial cloth. It's not your place to be involved in conflicts that don't concern you. Even if you are speaking the truth, your honest opinions may not be taken kindly. You will end up unnecessarily bringing other people's actions into your marriage if you stick your nose somewhere it doesn't need to be.

Similarly, keep your respective family members out of your married business, especially if your marriage has hit a rocky patch! It's easy for your families to take sides out of blind faith, even if they are wrong about the situation. Moreover, if the conflict ignites into an inferno, you may end up forcing your husband to choose between you and his family, and that is just not fair. Instead, make positive judgments to keep yourself in a positive mindset, and watch how God solves familial conflicts.

I come from a very large family that expresses love and comfort at all times, as does my husband, so I went into my marriage knowing the value of close familial bonds. Ultimately, I was able to nurture a close relationship with my husband's family, and he with mine. If you seek to destroy your husband's relationships with his family because you, yourself have a bad relationship with someone in his family, you are out of order! It doesn't matter how much you disagree with his family and their way of handling things. Always turn the other cheek. In other words, don't comment! Stop and think about how you can turn the situation into a positive one. I can hear you saying, "But his family is crazy and out of control!" But girl, you knew that already when you were upon the altar saying "I do." Proverbs 13:3 states "He that keepeth his mouth keepeth his life, but he that openeth wide his lips shall have destruction." Train yourself to keep your mouth closed and your tongue still. The time will come to speak your mind.

I find it interesting how many women do not hold their tongues because they think it is cute to talk loudly and be disruptive, embarrassing their spouses every time they are in public. I'm sure this issue destroys marriages daily. No one fights for their relationship anymore because they would rather hold onto their pride and let their tongues run loose. However, being a classy lady is like pouring expensive wine into a clear dollar store glass: It doesn't matter how cheap the glass looks because the wine inside is so divine and smooth that you cannot comprehend its expensive taste! This is why I have so much passion for mentoring the youth of today; they need someone to demonstrate how to be peaceful in the face of conflict. If you are a mother, I cannot emphasize enough the importance of teaching your kids to share positivity with the people around them so that your sons will know what to look for in women and your daughters will know what men expect of them.

Have you ever heard someone say of a woman, "She is beautiful both inside and out"? Or perhaps you have heard, "She really has it going on!" These compliments indicate the woman in question has a soul characterized by self-control and the ability to release unnecessary stress. She knows not only that she deserves respect but also the respect she should give to others. Here's the main thing -- she knows when to shut up!

You can be this kind of beautiful woman, too. This woman surrounds herself with positive people and strives to keep a peaceful mindset. She is a listener. She thinks before she speaks. Her natural aura of calmness and tranquility inspires radiance and beauty in all who surround her. Her light penetrates the entire room the moment she walks through the door. Women like her have boundless wisdom to share regarding handling disappointments, disagreements, and emotional pain.

My mentor was a woman like this. Her main statement to me was, "Love yourself and be true to yourself." This involves being willing to improve yourself so you can achieve the true potential locked within your soul. Yes, I am speaking to that woman who causes unnecessary arguments and controversy because she is unhappy with herself. What man wants to hear his wife continuously fuss about unnecessary issues? You must fully evaluate your thoughts before you speak and change your boastful character!

This fault is common in many career women, who feel they must step into bigger shoes to hold their own with the men in their workplace. If you are a professional woman working that 9-to-5 job, remember that the moment you step out from behind your desk and grab your purse to go home, you must leave that career woman persona at the office. Likewise, if you work from home, that businesswoman needs to log off the same time you log off your computer. Stop being the boss both at work and at home, ladies!

Often, your mouth can cause more hurt than you might realize. Learn how to keep things to yourself. Although there are undoubtedly men who are attracted to loudmouthed, mean-as-hell women, that is not the kind of man you want to attract, nor is that the kind of woman you want to be! These women build their relationships only so they can tear them down later and make themselves look good in the process. Ladies, I am instead asking you to clean your mouth because doing so will automatically cleanse your heart! With a clean heart and a clean mouth, you can plant good ground in your marriage that will bear good fruit. Once your marriage becomes balanced, God will pour rain upon you. With good ground, you can create a solid foundation, stable walls, and a sturdy roof, until no storm, tornado, nor heavy wind would be able to break you apart. The true mark of having built a steadfast relationship is when other young married couples start seeking you out for advice and direction.

All of that can be reached when you make up your mind to concentrate on yourself first and genuinely care about watching what you say. When your husband sees that you love yourself and respect others, he will eventually follow your peaceful spirit, but if you are conniving and sneaky or a liar or unwilling to change, nothing will save your marriage. That is why you have to clean your heart and mind before you say "I do"; otherwise, that selfish, self-centered, controlling monster inside of you will destroy your marriage. It is important to review your flaws and be willing to change. Ask yourself why you hold onto grudges and unforgiveness, and then work to overcome those flaws.

Ladies, we hold so much more power than we realize. Our spouses feed on our positive energy and emotions, but you must nurture that power to realize its full potential. If you struggle to stop and think before you speak, you must make it a priority to improve on that front. You must keep in mind that there's always a right time to speak and a right time to shut up!

Here are the ways you should strive to approach conflict with your husband, especially if you are prone to running your mouth or letting your temper take hold of you.

If your husband consistently acts in a way that upsets you, ask him why he feels the need to behave in such a hurtful way. Don't argue with what he tells you; just listen! He may storm off in anger or be unwilling to share, but eventually, he will come back to you, ready to vent about the reasons underpinning his behavior. In this way, by keeping the word "patience" front and center in your mind, you can strengthen your communication with him.

If your husband comes home and immediately starts nagging you, looking to pick an argument over something petty, remove yourself from his presence by going to another room and refusing to engage with him. Talk to him later about his actions when he has calmed down because your primary goal should be opening his eyes to his problem, not trying to win the argument he wants to pick. By engaging with him, you have already lost.

Study your spouse. Learn his habits and values so that you can understand where he's coming from when you argue. Assume he has good intentions, even if his execution and communication are poor at the moment. Approach him with empathy and kindness. Most importantly, try to compromise with him in these situations. All issues can be solved with patience and compassion.

Stop questioning and nagging your husband! You have to learn to trust him, especially if he is the type of man who won't immediately share the details of what is troubling him. Stop thinking about the worst-case scenario or ascribing negative motivations to him without proof. Ask him once, but after that, drop it! You won't gain further insight by bugging him with more questions.

Last but not least, examine yourself before pointing your finger at someone else. Our mouths can destroy our relationships in the blink of an eye. It doesn't matter if you wear designer brands or if you look like a supermodel or if you are the mother of his children; if you speak and think in a negative tone, he will fall out of love with you. You need to look at yourself in the mirror and ask yourself how to spin those negative thoughts into positive ones.

If you have ever stopped and asked yourself, "Why did I say that?" I have an answer for you: You are too used to letting words flow without a filter. It's your job now to find and install that filter! Only then will your marriage see growth and prosperity.

Here is the road map to shutting up:

1. Be watchful of your tone when you are arguing with your husband.

2. Don't speak thoughtlessly; take time to examine your heart and frame your words kindly.
3. It is not your place to butt into arguments that do not concern you.
4. "Shut up" may be a blunt phrase, but it is often the smartest action to take.

Chapter 8

What He Expects From His Wife

Men are mysterious human beings. They may share similar viewpoints on many issues, but they are different when it comes to the ones they love. Their mindsets change, and they are more focused on taking care of their households to ensure they leave inheritances for their loved ones. It is amazing how a man reverts to a being of dedication when his spouse is on the same dimension as him. If you are not on the same level, ladies, you must transform so he will follow you into God's arms. That is what he expects from you and loves about you, and he knows he can't do it without you!

We submit to God so we can learn to make our husbands better and help them release the stress that remains on their minds. Steve Harvey recently shared on his talk show, "My wife, Marjorie, is my rock because she takes care of what I don't know, and she helps me remember all these executives' names when I see them in public." See, she plays a crucial role in Steve's successful career: Not only does she take care of the household and the kids, but she also manages the minutiae of his schedule so he won't have worries in his heart as he brings home the dough. Know your position, ladies, as this will make a huge difference in your relationship. Can you imagine how amazing you will feel when you do what is right in God's sight? We can't change our men. Instead, we can change ourselves to make a difference in our relationships.

I often think about the women in this world who have been raised in difficult situations and the struggles they have overcome, how much strength they had, and how many tears they shed to move forward. Because these women had to learn how to succeed without guidance, they rebel against receiving direction. They don't have a clue what to do with love when they find it because they've spent their whole lives simply surviving. These women are so used to taking care of themselves that they don't know how to properly take care of their husbands.

If you're a woman like this, I'll tell you what you should do. You have to open up your heart and surrender to God. Watch God change your entire perspective and elevate you to the kind of wife He wants you to be.

Men investigate your whole family background on the first date because they want to ensure you can meet their expectations. They want to know whether you are educated and have the appropriate values if you keep in touch with your siblings, how any hardships in your past have shaped you, and if you have gained maturity from your struggles. Their goal is to investigate your mindset. Do your thoughts linger on drama from your past? Or are you able to let go and look to the future?

To any ladies who are still stuck in a time capsule, struggling to let go of poor choices from long ago – leave that mindset behind! It is time to push through the pain and regain control of your life so that your man knows he can depend upon you. That is what a man expects – a woman who strives to move forward and not backward.

I wasn't born knowing my husband's expectations of me, of course. I had to learn them as our relationship matured, but that's okay because he had to learn and meet my expectations as well. His expectations of me included cleaning the house, spending quality time with him, and cooking from time to time. My expectations of him included supporting me in achieving my goals and taking me on road trips.

But don't expect him to meet your expectations if you don't work hard to fulfill his! These are common expectations, ladies. Men expect women to cook sometimes! Cooking at home is healthier for you and your children, and being able to whip up a homemade meal makes you more attractive in many men's eyes. If he brings home the bacon, you better fry it up! Managing the housekeeping is important as well. A clean house reflects a clean mind and speaks to your commitment both to yourself and to your relationship. No man wants to come home after a long, hard day at work only to be greeted with dirty dishes and clutter everywhere! Living in a dirty house may be okay with you, but you shouldn't subject your husband to that.

I know what you are saying: "I work all day, and he's able to clean up, too!" However, we can easily make a difference in our spouses' lives just by doing what we know is right. It may not feel fair to you if he doesn't help with household duties, but someone needs to do it! You can tell him, "You expect me to keep the house clean and dinner warm, but I have expectations of you as well! We have to work together in all areas." If he doesn't respond to your words, don't stop fulfilling his expectations. Don't let his laziness bother you. He will meet you halfway eventually.

In the meantime, keep the house clean because the state of your home is representative of your reputation and lifestyle. Never settle for less. Can you imagine the things your friends and family are saying behind your back? If you always sport the latest fashions but they can't even sit on your toilet due to its funk? They see the clothes on the floor, the dirty dishes in the sink, dust everywhere, the kitchen counters, hidden under clutter and unpaid bills, and they whisper amongst themselves, "When she gets her paycheck, she must go to the mall and callously leave all her responsibilities behind."

You'll turn off anyone acting like this. People who see your dirty house won't care to ask if it's your fault or your husband's; they'll just see that you have fallen behind in your duties. Don't let your reputation take a hit just to prove a point to your husband! It isn't hard to be clean. It just takes time. So turn on some music and get to scrubbing. Get your husband involved by turning it into a team activity. It is such a turnoff when you are in good health but living in filth. There is no excuse for ignoring your environment and abandoning the necessary maintenance of your home!

To get your husband more involved in routine chores, create a schedule for both of you and commit to it. I'll tell you, weekends are an excellent time to do housework. Don't just waste your time being angry if your husband is not doing what you've asked him; instead, work with him to find a solution. Maybe you can hire someone; maybe he can put in more effort. Either way, you have to take over what isn't getting done around the house until he can figure himself out. Get yourself together, and do what needs to be done. Remember, cleanliness is next to godliness!

Let's keep talking about the word "clean," but this time in the context of hygiene. You would not believe how many women don't go to the doctor and dentist regularly. It's not that they don't believe in getting medical care; it's that they are afraid they will learn something is wrong with them. However, in the process, they let their hygiene and health go, and potential issues that could have been nipped in the bud escalate unnecessarily.

Men expect women to care about their precious bodies. A man loves a woman who looks good, smells good, attends her yearly medical exams without delay, and makes sure any issues are taken care of immediately. For example, if you have extreme body odor, talk to your doctor about it! Don't just complain about your aching joints without making any attempts to address the issue. There's nothing cute about having intercourse with your spouse while you're in pain or have an odor.

Similarly, when you don't go to the dentist, it shows on your breath! You are killing your man if you have an infected tooth abscess or painful cavity that you haven't fixed because you're ignoring the dentist out of fear. No matter how painful you think the dental procedure might be, I promise it's more painful for you and your husband to live with that problem tooth!

This is what your man loves about you: that you are a woman who values herself inside and out. So look in the mirror, review your body, and determine what needs extra attention. You've got to stay on top of your game, ladies because there are plenty of women out there who are on top of *their* game and won't hesitate to scoop up your man!

When I met my husband, I didn't realize that a man looks for his mother in his wife because his mother is the one to teach him what to expect from his wife. My husband had clear expectations of me when I met him thirty-six years ago, but it took me much longer – six years, indeed – to learn to meet those expectations and form my own expectations of him. It wasn't until I moved in with my husband, and we both learned about each other's perspective on life, that we were able to find common ground. Believe it or not, that takes *time*! That is how you learn what he expects from you and what you expect from him. Though this process can be lengthy, it will save your marriage by allowing you to discuss disagreements efficiently and clearly. Disagreements aren't necessarily bad; you simply have to go through them to achieve growth. Just remember what he expects and loves about you!

This next topic is a juicy one! Now, I must admit that I am still working on improving myself in this area, and I'm not doing as well as I'd like to. However, this is a necessary part of marriage. What am I talking about? Well, wearing lingerie!

Men love to see us wearing strings and sexy red shoes! I do not enjoy wearing lingerie, but he likes it, so this is important to my marriage. Ladies, I'm telling you, once you've been married as long as I have, you will run out of ideas to keep your intimate moments fresh! It is very hard to keep the bedroom ablaze. Listen, my God-fearing religious readers, you know that we have to satisfy our men in bed, and the bed is undefiled, so we already know that you are not making love to the hymns. Let your guard down and remain open.

If you are at a loss for how to keep your husband satisfied, don't hesitate to reach out to older couples who have reached those golden years together. Of course, they'll tell you to "keep God first in your marriage." Everyone's marriage journey is about learning and sharing with each other to reinforce their identities and become one with the body of Christ. That is why you should become friends before becoming lovers. Forming a connection will make your relationship more manageable and durable.

Divorces occur when you have both given up on meeting each other's expectations, especially in the bedroom. Women, we are stronger than men in this area because men's unchecked lust can easily talk them straight out of the decree of marriage. Men don't have a problem starting over in another relationship. They will simply carry what they learned in the first marriage into the second! And guess what, ladies… She will do what should have been done by you to keep your man happy! To prevent that, you have to force yourself sometimes to meet his sexual desires. Yes, it takes energy, but expending that energy is an investment in the future of your marriage.

However, don't run yourself dry or search for nonexistent energy deep within your soul just to bring joy to his heart. He may expect you to please him, but you should sometimes reserve your affection and use it to reward him for being a good husband. Make sure that you tell him why you are rewarding him so he keeps up the good work. We have requirements, too! Right, ladies? It's okay to stand your ground.

When I decide to set up a romantic evening with my husband, his response to me is hilarious. "Baby, what you doing? What! You in the mood for this?" It makes me laugh because he knows this is not my cup of tea. To tell you the truth, I am so behind on my reward game. I don't have an excuse. But I do know that it is a great way to spice up your marriage. My husband patiently waits for the next romantic evening because he knows it is a special treat, and this agreement keeps our love channels connected.

As women, we take the word "love" very seriously from our man! Love means a deep romantic or sexual attachment, an intense feeling of deep affection, a great interest, and pleasure. There are so many ways to express love to each other. An easy way to show your spouse you care about him is to be aware of how you conduct yourself in front of his friends. There are rules and regulations for making public appearances with your spouse. For example, you should never walk in front of him; walk beside him or an inch behind him, and let him open the door for you. Men expect their wives to be submissive and know their position, so it is good to be obedient and passive in public and at home. In this way, your aura will take over the room when both of you walk in. People will flock to you with questions regarding your relationship. Love will flow through the room in an instant and help countless hearts connect.

Be careful of whom you become when you invite your friends over for the game night, as well. Do you turn into a rip-roaring loud woman due to the influence of alcohol? You shouldn't feel the need to act like an impostor in your home, but you need to take control of the alcohol before it takes control of you. Know your limits so you won't embarrass him, or yourself. A classy woman will travel a long way in life, so you better learn how to have fun and laugh aloud while maintaining your class and dignity.

We all know what our husbands like to talk about with their friends. When men get together, they speak the truth to each other. They say what's in their hearts because they know they won't face any judgment. They sit back and advise each other freely, and they compare and learn from each other's situations so they can handle future arguments appropriately. Men can be very boastful about their wives – this is why I'm emphasizing the importance of handling yourself with respect and dignity around his friends.

More than that, though, most men enjoy not having to fuss or fight every day with their wives, and they love knowing their home is a haven to which they can escape after work. Your husband wants reassurance that you know your place and will provide what he wants before he even asks. If you keep him happy, he will want to keep you happy. It works both ways!

Here is the road map to meeting his expectations:

1. Fight for what you want, and don't let doubt cloud your mind.

2. Take good care of your body.

3. Do what is right, and honor your commitments.

4. Stay creative. Surprise him from time to time.

5. Make an effort to work as a team, even when times are tough.

6. Acknowledge that both of you have expectations of each other.

Chapter 9

The Season of Falling Out of Love

That's right, you read that title correctly! I am boldly stating that there is a season in marriage when you fall out of love with each other. If you haven't been told about this season, it will sneak up on you one day and slap you right across the face without warning! No one likes to talk about this subject because it is uncomfortable to explain that you have to expect the ride to get rocky. But do not jump out of the boat! Ladies, please keep in mind that we are peacemakers. Sometimes, when we know we are right and our husbands are wrong, it takes great humility to keep the peace no matter how mad we are.

It's a known fact that you will say to yourself one day, "I can't stand him! I don't understand what is going on in his mind." Then you start asking why you are feeling your relationship go up in flames, with past misunderstandings reappearing and angry arguments taking over every conversation. It's during this season that divorce rates skyrocket because one member of the couple may fail to walk through the dark tunnel until that miserable season ends.

Discernment plays a strong role in this season. It can be tempting to take the easy way out and get a divorce. However, valleys come in every relationship; it doesn't matter who you are with! No matter how miserable you begin to feel in this season, don't be the one who asks for a divorce; let him be the one to say that the marriage is over. Know that this is only a season, after all. You won't be here for long.

I've started looking at this season as a fresh start, where doubts and negative emotions are brought up again so they can be resolved, allowing love to blossom once more. The real problem is that some of us don't like change! We become content with the way things are going, but we need to remember that we should want more. This type of season escalates your life for the better.

Of course, the duration of the season depends entirely on the steps you and your husband take to replace that empty, lonely feeling in your hearts. I'll tell you now – action in the bedroom won't prevent this season from coming. This season comes when one of you reaches a new level in your endeavors and diverts all of your attention toward achieving your goals, leaving your partner feeling ignored and alone. This disconnect is further complicated because men are not good at communicating their emotions, especially when they suddenly find themselves in this season. However, the amazing thing is that you both have *nothing* to do with each other's shifting. You just happened to be the one chosen to walk beside him.

What I do know is that when life changes around you, it is a good thing! Change brings prosperity and amazing opportunities. However, it can be easy to let that change consume you. Marriages suffer through this season when whoever received the anointing of change stops being able to see anything else. That change becomes the sole target of their mind, and they think only about how to reach it in the shortest amount of time, even if that focus, along with the time spent researching and planning, comes at the expense of their marriage.

But if you remain strong, you will grow through this season! Remember that change is driven by purpose, and you will deal with it constantly throughout your marriage. In the process, it is important that you don't lose sight of the importance of keeping your love strong. The darkness of the tunnel makes it easy to forget that you are a team. It destroys your ability to communicate, causes you to point fingers for no reason, and makes you feel like it will go on forever. Your fear of the darkness will manifest as words that cause pain and prevent you from healing, and if you keep dwelling on negative thoughts, that season of lovelessness will camp around your marriage indefinitely.

Believe me, this is not a bad road to travel, because you are not alone; he's thinking the same things about you that you're thinking about him. There's a scripture in the Bible that can help put this season in perspective: *"Though I walk through the valley of the shadow of death, I will fear no evil: for thou art with me; thy rod and thy staff they comfort me."* (Psalms 23:4).This verse is especially apt due to the description of walking through a valley. In marriage, you will walk through as many valleys as you will crest mountains, simply because you are human, and humans change as they move forward in life. When you find yourself in one of these valleys, you can change for better or for worse. That is why it is important to find your purpose on this earth. Having that confidence will allow you to support your spouse and steer him toward his goals without resenting change whenever it comes into his life. Once you understand the importance of following your purpose, you will want to help him achieve his goals without any heartache or jealousy.

When your marriage reaches this season of falling out of love, try to keep the excitement alive, your mind focused, and your determination fully powered. It is easy for one partner in the marriage to feel as if he or she has been placed on the backburner. Don't let that unhappiness turn into a pity party! It takes patience, and support to climb your way out of the lowlands. When God shifts a marriage to a different level by nudging one partner toward their purpose, it is the other partner's responsibility to share creative ideas and support their spouse instead of getting upset about not receiving oodles of attention. That self-pity would drive anybody nuts! If you feel alone, back up and give your husband some room to think privately. Let him come around when he is ready to spend time as a couple. Ladies, he already knows what you are like, and that means he knows what the damn to do!

If you're thinking you can keep things the same as they are just by ignoring this season, I'm telling you that you're setting yourself up for disappointment! Change is a natural part of life, and this season is just another form of change. Though you may become frustrated, don't let it take over your mind and body. Instead, get ready to take action! You and your spouse need to involve each other in activities that you love doing together: walking through your neighborhood, riding your bikes, playing dominoes, cooking together, catching a movie you've been meaning to see. The goal is to achieve a positive, clear mind so you can get through these valleys. Having a clear mind will allow you to iron out the wrinkles in your relationship during this season without stress. When you find yourself struggling to climb the steep walls of that valley, dig deep within yourself to remember why you fell in love with him in the first place. That memory will give you the strength you need to keep placing one foot in front of the other until you reach the mountaintop.

And when you come together to fight for peace in your marriage, your love will be revealed to be true, just as you know *"that the trial of your faith, being much more precious than of gold that perisheth, though it be tried with fire, might be found unto praise and honor and glory at the appearing of Jesus Christ"* (Peter 1:7). Holding onto this faith is how you travel through dark tunnels and deep valleys in marriage. This is a season of learning, growing, and, most of all, renewing your mind. If you can hold tight through this season, the strong winds will eventually stop blowing, the storm will go away, and you and your husband will both be stronger for it.

My own marriage remained unstable for years because my husband and I married young, not knowing who we were or who we ever want to become. So when I realized my dream was to open a dance school for low-income families just as my oldest daughter was born, my focus shifted away from my household and toward my full-time job, and our marriage descended straight into a valley.

At that time, I wasn't mature enough to realize my focus had changed. In fact, it wasn't until my husband decided to focus on his own passion – opening a business that repaired trash compactors for corporations – that we noticed we were fighting to keep things together even as we chased individual growth.

However, what I thought was a valley in our lives became a testimony to the strength of our marriage and undeniable proof that opening this school was my life's purpose. Although I'm still in this valley, I know I'm leaving it behind soon, because my husband never stopped holding my hand, just like I held his hand through the process of opening his compactor business.

Ladies, the shortcut to solving this situation is to remain calm! Like I stated before, let the season take its course, and distract yourself by pursuing activities in your free time that keep you at ease. Just do what you are supposed to do and wait for him to come around. Valleys require a lot of prayer and time spent listening to that small, still voice inside of you. Do not let your heart dictate your mouth or convince you to take the wrong turn. This obstacle must be approached with care and creativity. So do what works, soothe his mind, and avoid stressing further over what has already been done. Everything that we go through will show its purpose in time – maybe not in our time, but surely on God's time.

Yes, we can survive that dark tunnel where lions prepare their attacks and storms gather. Stop saying to yourself, "I should leave this marriage," simply because you aren't willing to adjust your hardened heart. This kind of selfishness is what kills marriages. You cannot think only about yourself while ignoring your spouse's feelings and concerns. If you let selfishness settle in your heart, it will guide you right out of love by convincing you that what he feels no longer matters. Then you will start to disrespect him, and the whole relationship will crumble.

When you go through this season, remember to hang onto each other and watch how easily the blessings return to you. How many couples have missed this breakthrough because they refused to change to improve their situation? When you let problems come in like a hurricane, they will blow everything out of order, devastating your relationship, and creating countless hardships. Don't let this season erode your faith in your relationship. Spend time supporting your husband and children in their passions and endeavors, and remind yourself that family is what will carry you through this storm. Hold on tight and know that falling out of love only lasts a season. It is human nature. We have to step ahead and overcome this type of season in marriage to exchange our negative thoughts for victory.

Ladies, you will talk to God more than ever in this season when your mind is heavy with sadness and anger. You will stay at a confession mold, and your emotions will fly up and down like a roller coaster! But hold on tight, because the ride will be worth it, and the resulting growth will allow you to help others weather this storm of separate emotions. So many couples go to marriage counseling to escape this normal event, but there's no need for that. Keep a level head, and take your marriage one day at a time.

Once you and your husband have balanced your personal goals with your commitment to your relationship, use the strength you have gained to rebuild your marriage. Use what worked before to pull yourself out of the pit and shake that devil right off of you! We may experience plenty of struggles, but God knows we gain strength from them. This resulting strength guides us to a place where we can start over, and that is when we learn the most about each other. It is important to review your emotions so that you don't carry unnecessary grudges.

And once you've put this season behind you, this is what you do: Get dolled up in a cute dress and a nice pair of high heels. Spray some of that special perfume. Turn the lights down low and wait for him to come home. The love will reappear instantly once unnecessary distractions disappear from the atmosphere. Love can't live in a hostile environment; it can only survive in a peaceful environment. As long as your love for one another remains strong, you will be able to overcome this painful season. Replace your pain with passion and humility, and God will restore the rest.

Here is the road map to surviving the season of falling out of love:

1. Listen to your spouse, and support him in achieving whatever goals have drawn his focus.

2. Take time to meditate, regain your strength, and pray for him.

3. Don't let your emotions control you and lead you to the divorce court.

4. Listen to your intuition regarding the appropriate time to speak and to listen.

5. Replace lovemaking with other activities that you both enjoy.

6. There is a light at the end of the dark tunnel, so stay focused on walking toward it.

7. Let your pain inspire you to seek victory and turn your sorrow into joy.

Chapter 10

Pray For His Body, Mind, and Soul

Let me tell you what I am still learning: how to appreciate the king in my castle! I am learning the importance of covering him with prayer and appreciation by lifting him up to our Heavenly Father daily. We can get constipated with the mess in our hearts if we refuse to release the mess in our spirits.

My pastor is the best speaker on the importance of letting go. He sneaks it into his sermons from time to time, telling us we must learn to flush unnecessary mental blocks from our systems every day. Our minds and spirits must be clear if we are to pray for ourselves, our spouses, and our children. It is especially important that we, as wives, comfort, support, and pray for our husbands because they are not equipped to carry too much in their minds and hearts. Remember that although men are private human beings, they are incredibly sensitive as well.

Recently, I have noticed that when a man's wife covers him in prayer, he shines in every area of life and flows in abundance! His bank account explodes, and wherever he steps, the ground grows more fertile, and the fruits of his labor multiply. Ladies, you have to pray for him to stay focused on doing what is right for his marriage instead of letting his attention wander. Don't let him turn to the streets, where negative influences abound!

We have to stay involved in prayer to ensure the safety of our loved ones. Pray so that change will flow freely through their bodies, minds, and souls!

Stay woke! Keep your eyes on the people who surround your husband: his friends, his business partners, his mentors. Men who frequent the same social circles influence each other's characters and encourage personal development; unlike women, men are willing to compromise when they have conflicting opinions.

Now, I did not write this book about us ladies and our downfalls! Believe me, I am reaching out to married couples to share shortcuts you can take to move past bumps in the road. Don't make judgments hastily. Even if you move on to another relationship, these same trials and obstacles will follow you, so you might as well learn the necessary skills to deal with them now. Learn how to submit to your husband and keep his mind renewed his soul united with God, and his spirit connected as one. Yes, ladies, I am asking you to challenge yourself, but I guarantee it works! Extensively covering him with prayer requires effort, but the end results are miraculous! He will never be the same again. Healing will occur in his mind and his body, curing him of all sickness and disease, as God bestows favor in every area of his life.

As Bishop TD Jakes has stated, favor is not fair! However, this should not discourage you from praying over your husband and family. Our husbands depend on us to undertake the routine responsibilities involved in running the household, so it is up to us to be submissive and follow through on that expectation, or else we risk destroying what God has given us. If we only knew the percentage of divorces that occur because the husband suffered from having a dysfunctional wife with malicious intentions and behaviors... A woman with imbalances in her mind, body, and spirit can ruin a man's trust because men are not built to entertain immoral behaviors and impure thoughts. No, men are built to take care of their families and yield their minds and thoughts to the Lord. It would be devastating for a man to come home only to discover his wife hadn't been taking care of the household in favor of doing whatever she wanted.

Staying on the same page is vital in marriage. The closer you drive to Victory Street, letting all major circumstances and disputes pass you by until they are just specks in your rearview mirror, the longer the journey seems. I'll be honest with you, there are many days when I want to say, "Forget it. This is ridiculous." Even on those days, though, I know I have to stick around and handle the hardships because once I pass the Lord's test, I won't have to take it ever again! Once your husband comprehends the solution as well, you can cross that problem off your prayer list for good.

I suppose this is why God puts us through situations we can't overcome without Him. He knows that the fear of being stuck like this will force us to get our act together and ask Him for help. Men often insist on overcoming trials alone, but this stubbornness keeps them from reaping the rewards of the lessons God wants to teach them. That is why we pray for our husbands to hear that small, still, voice inside of them and walk where God leads them! The outcomes of their struggles will humble them.

Let's talk about something else now – vision. Prayers can only take you so far if you don't know what you're praying for, and this is where vision comes into play. So many of us are visionaries. We can see visions of things before they happen. When God blesses you with a vision of your future, channel the energy and clarity you have been given to make that vision come true! When it comes to building a successful marriage, you must first create the appropriate vision, and then you must picture that vision with an intention to see it manifest in reality.

This intentional act of turning visions into reality through prayer is what allowed my husband and me to find the perfect house to start our family in all those years ago. When we were preparing to buy our first home, we fell in love with the city of McKinney, Texas, but were unable to find a house there that matched both our budget and our wish list. As a result, we moved temporarily into an apartment in the southern area while we searched for a house in other cities. I guess God didn't want us in those other cities, though, because none of the houses we walked into had what we were looking for.

Near our apartment was a mansion with breathtaking wrought-iron gates, vibrant landscaping, and a kitchen that every wife dreams of cooking in. One Sunday, we stopped by the mansion, took a tour, and envisioned living in a house like this, never in our wildest dreams thinking that vision would come to pass. While we were there, the realtor showing the house stopped us and asked how he could help us, and, deciding we had nothing to lose, we told him we were looking for a home and gave him our names and number.

Three months later, that gentleman called and said he had found a home in McKinney that we might like. At this point, we had completely forgotten that we had prayed to live in this city permanently, but we realized that God had answered our prayers in His time. It had taken us more than a year to find our dream house, but we also would never have seen the house if we had not started dreaming big. That is when we realized the importance of making our visions clear to God; only then can He make them come true.

Ask yourself: Are you speaking your visions aloud? What are you doing to ensure your visions become reality? Are you speaking with your husband to make sure you're on the same page?

God rewards those who take care of what they have been given and maintain their faith. We may never understand why we have to undergo unexplainable pain, but we should focus on winning every battle we face and dreaming ever higher. When you and your husband work together to envision your victory, you cannot lose. That is why we have to pray for our connection as a team – this is how the vision we see for our families will smoothly come to pass. That is also why it is imperative to flush your mind and pray your husband will do the same. Instead of letting frustration fester in your soul, deal with one problem at a time, and think about all of your options instead of immediately giving up. Any time you want to say, "Bye Felicia," take a deep breath and kick anger out of your thoughts. This small change transformed my entire marriage because when my husband and I were creating our vision, he had no one to argue with but himself. Yes, you will have disagreements about the future you are building together, but you have to take control of your mind, body, and soul to collaborate on your vision. Once he sees you are approaching your joint visions with peace, he will crave that same mentality, and your visions (and marriage) will soar to incredible heights.

We have to do whatever is necessary to keep our commitment to the marriage organic and instinctive. Dedication is difficult, but it is rewarding! As civil rights activist Al Sharpton said, "If you just keep on going if you turn the corner, the sun will be shining." Keep moving toward your vision, and you will see the dreams of your heart and mind become reality. Don't be afraid to keep asking the Lord to show you the vision He has for your marriage! Even if you can't see that vision immediately, know there is a future for you that He will make plain in His own time. You cannot be impatient; He feeds on commitment and honesty. Just continue asking for clarity in every area of your mind.

Most importantly, maintaining your body, mind, and soul is important for your health. You will grow in aspects of your life you never noticed before if you keep your affairs in order. Remember to keep a teachable spirit because you never stop learning and growing. Stay hungry for your husband's healing and your healing as well.

I just love that word: "healing." We all need some form of healing somewhere. Marriage takes copious healing and forgiveness. Once you receive forgiveness for something, don't bring that trauma up again; moving on is a part of the healing process. Forgiveness prevents sickness and disease from building mansions in your mind, body, and soul.

People often say, "You can forgive but you should never forget," but I disagree. In marriage, you have to both forgive and forget to grow. I know you may not agree, but if you simply try to release the anger simmering inside you, your body will love you! We carry enough stress as it is; why add more when you can release it? Besides, your husband is watching you, to know how you handle hardships. If he knows you approach issues peacefully, that peace will transfer to his spirit and mind.

That desire to fight for your marriage is worth it! Did you hear what I said about desire? Desire is a strong feeling of wanting to have something or wishing for something to happen, and it is necessary for a strong marriage! If you lose that desire, you have lost your love for him. Desire lives in the soul of love and plays a vital role in marriage. When desire settles in your soul, it allows you to let go of any constipation in your mind and focus your devotion on becoming one with your spouse. Ladies, don't forget to continuously evaluate yourself to determine where you should seek change. Keep that log of love burning in the fireplace of your soul and your desire flowing like a stream.

Along with keeping your mind, body, and soul open to change and desire, you must pray for your husband to achieve peace of mind. If he envies your success or ambitions, he may lose his desire for you out of fear of being replaced or ignored. We need to be liberated from petty emotions like jealousy and stubbornness to be able to grow, and that requires trust! This kind of liberation becomes attainable when both of you open your minds to pursue your goals.

"Where the Spirit of the Lord is, there is liberty" (2 Corinthians 3:17). Freedom is never handed out; it must be earned through submission and commitment. We have to draw a line and firmly put an end to disrespectful behavior toward ourselves and our husbands. This can be difficult. After all, our souls are perceptive, and the resulting bond your soul forms with your husband's renders you both sensitive to the slightest unease or negative emotion. To gain liberation from the harms caused by negative emotions, you have to maintain a steady pattern of behavior.

Ladies, I've spoken about praying for his body, mind, and soul, but please apply this advice to yourself as well. You, not him, might be the one with the issues preventing your vision of marriage from becoming reality; you might be jealous and hard to please, or you might be the one refusing to give him freedom. Even if you think you couldn't possibly be at fault, stop and think about it! We have to clear our minds so that we can overcome any roadblocks in our way. Even with shortcuts, this journey toward Victory Street and successful marriage requires unquestioning obedience and faith from us ladies, but if we keep our eyes firmly on our final destination, we will reach the end of our trials without fail.

Here is the road map to turning your vision into reality:

1. Keep your eyes on the influences that surround your husband, and pray that negative influences speedily exit his life.

2. Ask God to heal your husband in every area of his mind, body, and soul.

3. Reject any negativity your husband expresses so that his mind will heal.

4. Keep your vision strong and explicit until it comes true.

5. Talk to your husband about your desire for keeping your marriage strong.

Chapter 11

Attract and Extract His Gifts and Talents

Has your husband ever come home and admitted to you he has been laid off or let go from work? He may have begun to freak out when he received that devastating news because he is the man of the household, and his concerns are to pay every bill and keep the refrigerator full.

It doesn't cross his mind why he may have lost his job in the first place. He may immediately assume the worst, believing falsely that hard times are coming instead of realizing that it is simply time for a change. Some men need to be extracted from their jobs so they can attract the kind of work God has directed them to do. I know, shifting careers is a terrifying move when you have mouths to feed, but it is good for the soul. We should never settle where we land in life; we need to continue searching until we find our life's purpose so we can experience true joy and happiness. Moreover, relationships benefit remarkably from experiencing the refreshment of realizing a purpose.

When you are waiting for your husband to overcome his fear and seek his inner talents, take the time to give him counseling and comfort. Advise him to look at the situation differently and review the gifts and talents within him, and then inform him that you will have his back if he wants to chase his dreams.

But keep in mind that when you agree to help him on this new journey, you are signing on to offer incredible sacrifices and support. You are pledging your personal time and patience to his service. You are committing to researching resources for him so he knows what next step to take. I am sure we know someone whose relationship has failed because they grew too impatient and didn't want to finish the journey. But we have to stand by our men when they face challenges.

As he wonders to himself, "What in the hell am I supposed to do now," you must step in! It is your job now to settle his stressful mind and encourage him to cast his net into the deep waters of his soul to seek the talents God has hidden within him. Using your intuition, you can coach him to become fully aware of God's instructions, and when God answers his prayers, even the ones he has forgotten about, you can help him understand clearly what has been unveiled. This type of revelation helps us hear the tick-tock of the Lord's clock! It's exciting and rejuvenates our faith. It takes a great deal for a man to jump by faith, but with your guidance, he will see this is the road he has to travel.

Show your husband that trying again is not simply an option, it is a *mission*. We have all been given gifts to help us fulfill our missions in life, and if we decline to acknowledge those gifts, then we have chosen to forsake our happiness and the legacy we ought to leave for our children. Your husband must leave behind his anger and strive towards his goals because we all have to believe in something and not settle for less.

Honestly, the word "less" bothers me. It has such negative implications. Take "Payless ShoeSource," for example – yes, you pay less, but the shoes also wear out quickly. Similarly, so many men settle for less, remaining content with jobs that don't challenge or value them appropriately. Your husband needs to understand the empowerment that comes from breaking the chains of contentment and fighting for his dreams. You have to help him recognize his worth before it slips away from him, or else he'll suddenly look up one day, shocked by how much time has passed while he kept his head down, content.

I assure you he knows he is not receiving the compensation or appreciation he should from his employer. However, I can also assure you that he is scared to extract himself from that situation and move on to better things. Instead, he talks himself into settling for less to avoid the stress and pain that come with chasing prosperity. It's not easy to jump into the deep ocean where God does great miracles, and it's harder to remain still underwater until the breakthrough arrives. Men want to know how long the Lord plans to take because they're constantly busy, hustling, and bustling to earn an income and provide for their household.

This is where you come in. You have to extract your husband's drive-by force and explain to him that change takes time, but meanwhile, he needs to keep traveling down the road to success. Don't let your man settle for less or give up on the journey he has started! Offer him guidance, and teach him to inhale the knowledge and advice that the good Lord has given him for free! Help him maintain a positive attitude, and direct his energy towards the end goal, regardless of whatever obstacles come his way. These obstacles want him to fail. They want him to be overcome by pain and agony and stop in his tracks because they know that once a man gives upon himself, it can take him a long time to get back on his feet. In these situations, you must convince your husband to reach out for help, even though his pride may prevent him from doing so. Surely you know someone who can mentor him through overcoming these obstacles.

Moreover, you can help your husband generate the proper mindset for chasing his goals and accepting the Lord's direction by encouraging him to spend a few minutes each day with the Lord. Working prayer into his daily routine will rejuvenate him and open his mind to the Lord's will. If he is stressed over his work or providing for the family, dedicating some time to prayer will recalibrate his energy levels and remove the stress from his mind.

Getting your husband to attain this inner peace and joy should be your ultimate goal because when your husband is happy, your marriage will launch in a whole new direction. This has been my goal since I married my husband. He has been working hard since the age of thirteen, never failing to provide for our family even when we were struck by hard times. To help him avoid burnout, I encourage him to speak with God for ten minutes every day for direction. The difference I have seen in him is tremendous, and I can only imagine how much this will benefit our marriage as he continues to travel toward achieving inner happiness!

Another obstacle your husband may encounter on his journey toward greater success is jealousy. This is a hard spirit to deal with because it doesn't allow you to believe in yourself. It wrongly tells you that you will never achieve the same success as the people you're observing. Men often struggle to recognize their own value when they see others whom they perceive to be better off, and that insecurity manifests as toxic jealousy and cutting sarcasm. If you see your husband struggling with this issue, and it is getting in the way of him chasing his passions, you have to fight the good fight to beat that spirit back!

Explain that the rejection he fears will only make him stronger and that he must use this fear as motivation to work harder instead of as an excuse for giving up. As I mentioned in chapter 3, your mission is to boost his ego. It is a difficult job, but you will be rewarded eventually when he understands his worth and you see the fruits of your labor. Until then, just do what you are supposed to do, and don't worry about anything else.

You will see his mind clear as he realizes there is a light of success at the end of this tunnel of hardship. The same measure of faith has been given to all of us. We have to encourage our spouses to believe in their dreams no matter what other people think. When your husband finally begins to believe his dreams are worth chasing and that he can do so, he will overcome the jealousy rotting in his heart and achieve mental stability.

Promoting mental stability inspires a desire to strive toward greatness, so determine the areas where he is insecure, and then grab those negative thoughts and pull them right out of him! He won't know what hit him! Pray directly for what you need, and know that

God will answer your prayers in time. Meanwhile, help your husband remain motivated and on the course to victory. I know this is much easier said than done, and you will endure many tears and long nights, but everything will come to fruition in time.

Listen, we were made to stand strong in the face of the forces that work against us. We are helpmates: We help make the decisions when our husbands get confused! If you have to help him find solutions, make sure you approach him with a clear plan of action, because giving him a clear understanding of the problem and his role in fixing it will make it easier for him to act. Every little bit of your help or advice will lead him closer to completing his mission. He may not tell you "Thank you" in so many words, but know that you have done your part, and he will never forget it!

Get him to analyze the special effort it takes to get inside the door. Help him open his eyes and show others that he is a millionaire, too! We are all millionaires! Once he discovers his mission in life and begins running toward it, his gifts will open up that millionaire door, and no one will be able to close it but God. However, once he steps in, you must make sure he maintains the character to keep it open. Don't let the power of success change him! Keep him grounded in reality by reminding him that his success can be taken away at any time. At the same time, encourage him to give back to others; after all, someone helped *him* reach his goal, so he ought to pay that kindness forward by helping someone else fulfill their mission. This is what life is all about: Give and it shall be given back to you!

Ladies, if you have found yourself in a situation where your spouse is debating whether to go for his dreams, you know what you need to do. Inspire him to carry out his mission instead of procrastinating and wallowing in self-doubt. There is no time to waste! Yes, extract him from his stagnant circumstances and attract the gifts and talents hiding within him! Stimulate his interest in his goals, excite him about where he is going, and explain that it takes effort and determination to shape a vision into reality. Be trustworthy and dependable.

If you use the shortcuts I have shared with you, you, too, can help your spouse successfully commit to his dreams. I am a true believer of, jumping into the deep waters with only God's guidance – just ask my family! I have been doing it for years, and He hasn't failed me yet. In the words of Tyler Perry, "It doesn't matter if a million people tell you what you can't do, or if ten million tell you no. If you get one yes from God, that's all you need."

Here is the road map to attracting your husband's gifts:

1. Believe that your gifts and talents will take you far.

2. Refuse to simply be content. Don't settle for less.

3. There is a million-dollar door out there with your name on it!

4. There is no room in your marriage for jealousy.

5. Know your worth, and don't stop until you reach your goal.

Chapter 12

Forgiving Him for Cheating Can Be a Challenge

Though I hope you never have to ask yourself this question, you may find yourself having to determine whether you should forgive your spouse because he has cheated on you, or you may know someone who is going through this situation. It is a painful question, so let's talk about it.

No one likes to feel pain, whether physical or emotional. When your husband cheats, the pain you feel settles inside your heart. You may feel that your husband has caused you too much pain to even think about forgiving him. However, you made a covenant to stay with him for better or for worse. Well, ladies, this is the "worse"! Even if you don't want to, you know you should give your marriage a second chance; the reward of moving past this obstacle will make up for the effort. Don't think that you are saving the marriage to remain in a haven. No, you are working to move past this obstacle because God's unpredictable favor opens up many doors when it comes to obediently fight for your marriage.

As I mentioned in chapter 5, time heals all pain. But in the meantime, living with pain is no game! When pain takes root in your heart, it takes away your inner beauty and makes the world seem darker. That is why it is so important to forgive without keeping track of other people's offenses! The majority of us think we have forgiven and forgotten, but we continue to revisit that betrayal. Holding the memory of the pain inflicted on you prevents that pain from leaving your heart and hinders total forgiveness.

It is becoming more and more common for married partners to slip in their devotion to God and break the covenant of marriage by resorting to adultery. By engaging in this act, one is fully exhibiting free will and choosing to break the covenants to both God and their spouse. Although surrendering to the spirit of lasciviousness may feel good at such a moment, there is always a price to pay.

I want you to take a moment to step into your husband's shoes and think about why he fell victim to temptation. Why was he vulnerable to desire? Why was he dissatisfied with what he already has? There's always a reason behind our actions. Even if we are attracted to others, we have control over our behaviors, so why did he lose that control?

The goal of this chapter is to explore different points of view and how to approach them. After all, we are only human, and we all make mistakes. But rebuilding the love you and your husband share is vital. Once you lock that love in, forgiveness becomes paramount, and no bad situation should have the power to destroy your relationship.

Although we are all led to forgive, women, in particular, need to offer forgiveness without hesitation because doing so will yield many rewards in our personal lives. God places a ram in the bush when we choose to make the right decision, even if we dislike doing so. And forgiveness is a choice – a choice we should make every time.

I struggled with forgiveness for a long time, whether that meant forgiving myself for not chasing my dreams or forgiving the children who bullied me in my youth. I kept asking myself, why am I hung up on the bad things when something good has always followed? You should ask yourself this question also. Refocus your mind so you can examine the situation from another angle, and remain patient, allowing clarity and healing to manifest in time. That change in perspective can help you understand the importance of forgiveness.

Another point to consider is the role our conscience plays in our lives. Some people subscribe to the theory that your conscience is simply your moral compass, while many maintain that your conscience is the Holy Spirit guiding you. Regardless of which camp you fall in, you must ask yourself: Can you trust your conscience? Are you obedient to your conscience? Our consciences speak loudly because they play a powerful role. They serve as a line of communication between our souls and God. The conscience doesn't give incorrect guidance because it has a spiritual radar that sends warnings when we stray too close to immorality.

Other people may think we are being stupid when we give others second or third chances, but we must remember that our consciences guide us correctly in the face of devastating situations. Don't worry about how other people judge your decisions. Your resultant healing will soon prove the importance of forgiveness. Your conscience protects you and serves as a reminder that God is always working on your behalf. Trust your conscience to openly receive God's final authority. Healing doesn't happen suddenly; you have to keep an open heart and mind and give your conscience time to fight its battles. Don't wrestle with your conscience when it is visibly giving you signals. You will be covered with God's grace when you honor God's covenant.

Meanwhile, fight for what you want, and just keep going, knowing that goodness is right beside you.

Keep in mind, your trauma is your treasure, and no man can take that away from you! When your heart has been traumatized by the one you love, it pushes you to strengthen yourself and regain your emotional stability. With each traumatizing incident, you become stronger and more resilient, until you and your heart can battle even the strongest of conflicts that may befall you. Unexpected troubles will cross your path for as long as you are alive on this Earth, so just keep living!

When you find yourself having to choose between your pain, anger, or hurt and extending forgiveness, keep in mind that goodness and mercy follow you through life – but only if you are gracious yourself. If you become stuck in a place of un-forgiveness, step back, breathe, and don't make any radical decisions. Ignoring your conscience in a time like this will ultimately lead to regret. Think about how many people are incarcerated because they reacted irrationally in the face of their spouses' mistakes and took matters into their own hands. If you asked them why they flipped out instead of stepping away, I guarantee they would tell you their actions were the result of severe hurt.

Once you have gripped this wisdom, you will be able to determine the soundness of action and enact the principle of peace! You will be able to crush the serpent's head and attain victory in your marriage. When healing the wounds of your heart, you have to remember the vision of marriage that you saw when you first fell in love with him. Think about how many times our first love, God, has forgiven us, and channel that same strength of forgiveness. As Grammy-winning gospel artist Israel Houghton wrote, "Go back to your first love / go back, return / and let the fire burn again." Staying connected to our first love is crucial; this is how you forgive someone who has hurt you unnecessarily. When God is your first and primary lover, your love will outweigh every mental and physical barrier.

So stand your ground and fight for your marriage rather than doubting it or preventing it from moving forward. So much has come to the natural realm from the spiritual realm to strengthen your resolve and convince you to hold onto your marriage. Don't give up without returning to your first love and asking Him to transfer His wisdom to you.

If your marriage has been corrupted by this evil sin, it is okay to ask God why. This kind of sinful disruption can come from anywhere; all it needs is an open space. It creeps up on us unexpectedly and grows, unnoticed until it is too big to ignore any longer. Throughout your marriage, Satan will make many unavoidable attacks! And there's no other choice but to get through it. Ask God why you are facing these trials, but make sure you follow that question with a request for God to guide you to victory.

It took me a long time to release all of my stress and allow God to fight my battles. However, I eventually learned that if you ask Him to help you fight the battle of learning to forgive, He will! The Bible says that *"Wisdom is before him that hath understanding"* (Proverbs 17:24). When a man has an understanding, he is of an excellent spirit. If your spouse asks you to understand why he did what he did, try to receive his words with an understanding of your own, so you can ask God to handle that battle for you. You will have good days and bad days in your marriage, so admire the good days and let God fight your battles on the bad days. Keep your eyes on the ultimate goal of being a virtuous woman. We have the power to make everything all right because we are peaceful spirits. When we carry peace, we make peace in all forms of the situation.

Ultimately, being married is hard work and requires forgiveness of some sort daily! So sweep all the dirty crumbs of life into the dustpan, and throw them away before preparing yourself for the next set of dirty crumbs being scattered in your path. Don't be disgusted by the dirty crumbs because that is when the heart rejects forgiveness! Don't give up so soon, and don't remind one another of your faults. Instead, give each other space and time for redemption. It is important that you learn to forgive to save your marriage.

Here is the road map to forgiving and forgetting:

1. Fill your heart with forgiveness so that you can forget his misdeeds.

2. Forgive him because that is the Lord's will.

3. Don't give up so soon; trauma to the heart is a treasure.

4. Trials and tribulations target the heart but strengthen your resilience.

5. This battle is not yours; it is the Lord's.

Chapter 13

Learn How to Celebrate Yourself, By Yourself

None of us are perfect. However, we have all been wonderfully made by God. Therefore, I want to talk to you ladies about honoring yourself. Men love strong women who know exactly what they bring to the table. This type of woman goes back to school to expand her horizons, she mentors, other people, to help them achieve their goals and volunteers with charitable organizations to give back to the community. Because of her level of self-assurance, she can respond to her husband with positivity no matter what he screams about! When you learn how to celebrate yourself, you communicate to your husband that you can handle any trial with strength and courage.

There are plenty of self-confident women out there who have made a point of celebrating themselves and living happily. However, many women are afraid to live freely or on their own. I was one of the latter when I was younger. Before I met my husband, I had never lived alone, and I couldn't imagine how I would cope with it. However, as I grew older, I learned how to be content with my own company. I am going to share my journey toward that contentment with you so you can start your own journey.

You cannot lean on neighbors and friends to celebrate you. You have to celebrate on your own! This means learning to enjoy your own company and tackling the challenges in your life with grace. It is like you are dating yourself: taking yourself out for dinner alone, bonding with the people around you, and working to improve your weak areas. We all face trials and experience pain, so we have to learn how to grow from those experiences and move forward. When you overcome an obstacle, celebrate yourself for accepting what you couldn't change and moving past that obstacle with strength and faith!

Self-love starts with understanding yourself inside and out. Look in the mirror and ask what is holding you back from becoming the best, most confident, and motivated version of yourself. Then take a sheet of paper. On one side, write down the things you don't like about yourself. On the other side, write down the things you love about yourself. For both lists, think about more than physical appearances; dig deep inside yourself to find your innate qualities. Once you have created both lists, examine them with a gentle but unbiased eye. The list of shortcomings identifies what areas you need to rectify so you can feel proud of who you are and stand tall in the face of unexpected attacks. At the same time, the list of positive qualities serves as a reminder that you are worth celebrating. You may have flaws, and you may have made mistakes in the past, but these things shouldn't stop you from loving yourself and celebrating your accomplishments. You have that resolve inside of you that will allow you to do what needs to be done! The more you grow, the stronger you will need to be, because you can easily lose yourself in the process of breaking into this new dimension.

That exercise is what allowed me to finally enter the next dimension of my life. I have a learning disability that makes it difficult for me to comprehend vowel sounds. My daughters still help me with pronouncing words correctly sometimes! But despite their constant love and support, I have faced challenges due to this disability, and I have battled insecurity in many instances. For a long time, I didn't feel like I could write this book, and I'm sure that I have missed out on many other opportunities because my disability was holding me back. Throughout my life, I cried out to the Lord, asking Him why I had to fight so many battles and why it felt as if I was fighting all these battles alone.

However, when I listed out my positive and negative traits, I noticed that even while fighting these battles, I was able to bring joy to others and encourage them to activate their faith, whether through my songwriting or my dance school or my duties as a mother. That was when I realized God was guiding me through these battles so that I would develop the strength to share my gifts with others. I had to learn to love and accept the gifts He had given me and move forward through the pain. When I fully embraced the truth of who I was, I moved into a new dimension where I was able to celebrate myself and continue my journey toward Victory Street. Now I arrange songs for developing artists, and I am also an author. But it took years of fear, tears, and deep soul-searching to retrieve my revelation.

Celebrating yourself isn't easy, but it's necessary! Think about this process like climbing a mountain: Success is not measured by how high you have climbed but by how many times you push on and how far you get without giving up. When you understand that celebrating yourself is about making the journey rather than summitting the mountain, you will suddenly find yourself reaching your goal anyway. Keep moving forward until you reach your goal.

My husband has a saying about this as well: "Just keep throwing shit against the wall until something sticks!" I love that phrase! What he means is you need to keep fighting for what you want and refuse to stop until you make it! As long as you continue moving, you will have something to celebrate.

When you start growing in life and loving yourself, you will see the "fruits" of life appear, and your fruit will be visible to others as well. That fruit matures due to you loving yourself and sharing your fruit with others who come to you for advice after seeing the bright light and radiant glow of peace shining within you. It can be difficult to adopt this mindset if you are used to pleasing others instead of putting yourself first. However, when you try to keep others happy at the expense of loving yourself, one day you will look up and realize you have lost yourself.

For example, when I was younger, I used to go roller skating weekly with my girlfriends. I was awesome on those skates! But when I married my husband, I had to devote all my time to the housekeeping and taking care of our kids, and my roller skating hobby fell to the wayside. A few years ago, I decided to start skating again. To my dismay, when I placed the skates on my feet, I could barely stand up! I hadn't kept up my skills in roller skating for all those years, so I lost it all!

It's the same situation when you set your personal growth aside to focus on others: You will lose it all! You don't realize that you have settled for less than whom you are supposed to be. It is important to reinvent yourself from time to time to keep yourself feeling unique. Go to the mall and buy yourself something new, or book a session at the spa to release the toxins from your body. Have a ladies' night out where you all laugh together and gossip about the latest fashion trends. Watch a movie by yourself and indulge in popcorn *and* candy.

Setting aside personal quality time allows you to speak with God as well. You can open up to Him about your worries and give Him full control of the situations in your life that need to be handled. When you pass your stress to God, you are left with a sound mind that allows you to confront difficulties with grace. That sound mind directs your every move on this earthly realm and keeps your faith in motion.

So stop and learn what makes you who you are. Share the things that make you happy with your husband. Ignore any suggestions from your girlfriends or family that go against what you know to be true about yourself; what matters is what makes you happy. You are a winner and don't you ever forget it!

Knowing you are a winner in the deepest part of your soul is a sign that you love yourself and that you celebrate yourself. It is not an act of arrogance; it is an act of confidence. Though I knew objectively that I was a winner, I had to search my soul for what made me feel like a winner. What made me feel good about myself? When I knew the answer to that question, I stopped settling for jobs that didn't fit me and focused on chasing my dreams.

Because here's the fact of the matter: Winners fight and don't quit fighting until they reach the top. You already had everything you needed to be a winner and a confident woman worth celebrating before you met your husband. And he knows that, too! Men fall in love with women who know themselves intimately and deeply. Men want to be with women who have their eyes set on where they are going in life. Women who love themselves experience a natural flow of life, and others – both men and women – see that about them.

Ladies, you will achieve your potential as winners once you accept who you are unconditional. That's the hard part! So many of us don't love ourselves enough to continue moving toward Victory Street. Victory Street has been my goal for a long time, and all my friends and family know this about me. I believe that we are all connected to a victorious life; we just have to determine where Victory Street is located for us, and that means keeping our spirits open to the Lord's guidance.

For a long time, I thought my personal Victory Street revolved around my complete dedication to God and to raise my children as devoted Christians. Then God opened my eyes to what Victory Street means to Him. The revelation of this ultimate goal was so strong inside my spirit that I found myself riding blindly for years to chase down what God was telling me. I pursued dreams and visions of this street for decades until I was forced to discover myself and learn my life's journey and purpose. This revelation was a breakthrough not only for me but also for my entire family!

Listen, ladies, you have been placed on this Earth to submit to your husband, and you will receive incomparable rewards when you incorporate your wisdom into the lives of yourself and your children. Love yourself and keep your mind on Jesus! Celebrate your deliverance and freedom, because we are free to enjoy life and what God has given us. Remain positive so your love can flow without blockage. When you learn the deepest truths about yourself, God makes all things anew, and you don't have to be concerned about where He is taking you.

Let's say it together: We can achieve victory! Anything that isn't designed to aid you in moving forward must go. Exchange that life of pettiness and jealousy for victorious living. Learn how to stay out of other people's business, and don't make small issues heavy on yourself. Take time to explore life alone, and dress up occasionally to remind yourself that you are sexy. Periodically refresh and renew everything about yourself because making new choices is a simple and marvelous way to seek growth. Your goal is to love yourself to the extent that painful experiences are unable to control your attitudes. It is a straight-up turn on for your husband when you are secure and comfortable with your own self!

While clearing out your personal junk, remember to nurture your spiritual belief as well. You can't receive spiritual contact and passion if you are not connected to God. I have experienced that supernatural passion with God on several occasions, and those encounters taught me to love myself unconditionally. Accepting who you are, gives you a feeling of completion. It is an experience that I can't explain, but you will know when you have it. It's not deep, ladies. It is a relationship. If you search your soul earnestly and are wholly prepared to make the necessary changes, you will find that your radiance will inspire others to love themselves as well.

Be grateful for what you have, and willingly share with other women what it takes to celebrate yourself. It is utterly rewarding to see your friends begin to focus on where God wants to take them, and it is unimaginably satisfying to speak healing into their spirits. Stop running in the dark, chasing what you cannot see. Instead, look for the exit signs that will direct you toward Victory Street!

Today, I celebrate the strength God placed in me to withstand His tests. Stand up and clap if you are ready to make the changes necessary to begin celebrating yourself! And if you have already traveled this road, congratulations on the progress you have made toward Victory Street. Either way, when you begin to breathe in peace, joy, and happiness, you will experience the comfort of living and loving life!

Here is the road map to celebrating yourself:

1. Fight for your fruit to manifest inside of you.

2. Welcome to the new dimension of your life.

3. Love yourself so you can love others.

4. Meditate on what makes you smile.

5. Focus on achieving victory so you can live a prosperous life!

Chapter 14

He's Not Ready Yet! But Transformation Will Come

It is important to mold yourself into someone who can stand steady through transitions and face any opposition from your husband when he is not ready for change. When your husband opposes the change, you must work with him to overcome that resistance and get him to surrender to his fears so that he can identify what is keeping him from giving 100 percent of himself to your relationship. You have to stomp on the head of his opposition before it has a chance to drag you both down with it, especially if that opposition arises from his own struggles. Overcome difficulties with grace, knowing that you have to stand firm against your husband's reluctance until he is ready to move past it and release his problems and fears.

Men face abundant opposition both at work and at home. In dealing with that opposition, they may be misdirected by dirty-minded friends or swayed toward the comfort of alcohol. It takes a lot of prayers to handle a man who is dealing with a dirty mind, but the good news is that if he loves himself enough, he will be willing to transform into a better man forever.

So keep planting the seeds of greatness into your marriage without worrying whether those seeds are landing in good soil or bad soil. If you continue watering the seeds, the soil will transform into good ground. The beast of sin sits ready to push your husband toward sin and addiction, but you are here to oppose the beast and keep your husband pointed toward Victory Street.

In this chapter, let's talk about the transformation that is yet to come! This transformation will turn your husband into that new man you have been patiently waiting and praying for. Wait for this transformation with tranquility and a calm disposition, and avoid unnecessary uproar by handling your spouse with a soft tone. Your kindness will play a huge role in your man's transformation.

Instead of nagging your husband to change, demonstrate what it takes to achieve that transformation, and obtain harmony. Remember, the goal is to keep his compass straight so he doesn't go off track. Once he tastes harmony in the relationship, he will hunger for that sweetness forever, making it easier for you to keep that momentum while he is undergoing dramatic change.

But be warned: This isn't a straightforward journey. You will experience weekly meaningless fights because of his unwillingness to embrace change and prepare for the obstacles life has placed in his path. When he opposes that transformation within himself, no one can change his mind but God! At times like this, you will find yourself replaying the crazy, rude, hurtful statements he has made toward you, and you will ask how he could say those things to someone he loves. But you need to know that he only says those things to feel good about himself! He maligns your character to uplift his spirit and justify his wrongdoings! It becomes easier to cope with his angry statements if you remember that he is swimming in contempt and disgust for himself born of his unwillingness to make a change.

You can look at men today and see from their external appearance whether they have accepted their transformations. A man who has been transformed eagerly devotes his time to charitable causes and personal growth. Even the lowest educated man can become a lion if he manages to orient his compass correctly! Transformed men keep climbing until they reach the top of the mountain! Maybe these men don't believe in themselves at first, or maybe they think no one else cares about them, but when they identify the strength they carry, they don't hesitate to apply it to their ambitions and goals. They know they have nothing to lose by chasing transformation! It seems like these men accept change more quickly than men who think they already know everything necessary to accomplish their goals.

No matter how confident your husband is, though, sooner or later you will face hard times. It is difficult for men to fight through these trials, especially if they have encountered similar hardships in the past. Battling the storms of change is no cakewalk for women, but men have significantly more trouble with it. Every little change has to be examined methodically, and every little detail must be thoroughly understood before he can incorporate that new information into his next move.

For example, consider the changes that come with aging. Women can embrace aging on their own terms because there are a plethora of skin and hair products available for women to alter their appearances. The majority of men, however, simply wash their faces and brush their teeth and get on with their day! When age starts to change their appearance, there is little they can do to reverse time. Consequently, some men feel as though they lose their masculinity when they age because they uphold their outward experiences as a hallmark of their masculinity, making it difficult for them to embrace that natural change in their lives.

Although you and I both know that aging is beautiful and that men who embrace transformation age gracefully and don't carry hard times on their faces, this path is not easy for men to travel. Often, men worry that they will lose everything without gaining anything, or that they will miss out on opportunities that are only available in youth, and to avoid feeling left out of these experiences, they retreat into a dark tunnel of denial! Once inside this tunnel, many men cannot focus long enough to find the exit, so they run themselves to death while refusing to accept change and release the fears that have been strangling them for so long.

However, we, their wives, are here to guide them along the path of change. With your help, your husband will not succumb to the darkness. He will instead take a deep breath and press on toward the light. You will travel through countless dark tunnels in your marriage, but if you hold his hand and guide him patiently, you both will be winners! Life may burden you with difficult times and insurmountable changes, but press on through that dark tunnel, and watch your husband's transformation begin.

Now, once he is willing to undergo the transformation he needs to reach salvation, he will be ready for whatever comes his way. He will set aside the jealousy that plagues him and seek support in embracing the truth. To nourish his soul, he will soak up positive messages. Most importantly, he will understand that the beast of sin deliberately endangers him, and as a result, he will examine what comes to harm him so he can take the proper protective measures, not only for himself but also for his family and friends. When he reaches this level of change, impress upon him the truth that he is an example to his peers! The change within him will rejuvenate and revive the people around him.

Another effect of this transformation is that your husband will realize that mistakes and fights will not lead to ruin! Whatever poor outcomes his actions have caused can be reversed. The word "ruin" is like a marinade for a piece of steak: If you leave the steak to soak in the marinade overnight, you wouldn't expect it to still taste bland when you cook it the next day! Similarly, if you let your husband's spirit soak in the word "ruin," it will affect his mindset and color his view. When you believe and accept that something is ruined, you also accept that it can never be replaced. Well, I am telling you that nothing in our lives is ever ruined. Poor circumstances simply become available for reform. Your marriage is the same way – not ruined, just waiting to be reformed. This transformation will show him that his physical destruction brings suffering upon him, and that is when he will realize that his transformation was worth fighting for.

Once you have removed the word "ruin" and its accompanying negativity from your life, I want you to carefully think about what has been left behind for you to pick up and rebuild. Your husband may have deep wounds from his youth that he thought were ruinous until he received his transformation, and, now those wounds have reopened so the healing process can begin. They are ugly wounds, painful wounds, but if he has accepted his transformation, his salvation will strengthen him and teach him not to fear failure. God will revive his dry bones and call them to move again! His salvation will cloud out the sinful thoughts and actions that submerged your husband's life in turmoil and blocked off every escape and avenue for blessings to enter his home. That is the power of the praying wife: Your efforts will buck up his resolve and allow him to win every battle, shirking off the junk he has been lugging around his whole life that has prevented him from undergoing that radical change.

On the other hand, nothing will encourage a man to run full speed ahead toward transformation more than a woman who is disorderly in her ways! This kind of woman reveals her Jezebelian tendencies shamelessly and without remorse. Everything about her, from her breath to her thoughts, is evil and driven only by self-gain. She would stomp over her loved ones without hesitation and then fold them into a hug, no matter how much she has hurt them because she wants to ensure that everything in her life goes her way. She must be the only one left standing in her man's life so that all his attention is given to her alone.

No matter what form of relationship this hazardous woman is committed to, she believes the light must shine on her at all times. She displays these selfish actions fiercely because she thinks she holds all the cards in her hands. She believes her husband is blind as a bat and has made no provisions for the aftermath of her fall. Yes, that's what I said: her fall! There's no way a woman with that dark a heart will get away with her devilish ways, her inner secrets, and her egocentric scams, and she knows it! She will make sure there is a cushion for her fall but will leave her husband hanging high and dry without any hesitation.

Ladies, if you are this type of woman who puts her desires above all else, you must seek your transformation before you help your husband with his! Maybe you are running from the wounds of your past, and you are unintentionally inflicting the same pain you have felt yourself on the people around you. The consequence of this is that everything you have built with your husband is on pins and needles! Nothing is solid and ready to be built upon by your children. When you have driven everything to ruin, you will leave behind your unresolved wounds and hatred, lingering in the atmosphere like smoke from a campfire.

In the meantime, his transformation will clear his vision like you can't imagine! With a soft smile, he will track every move you make and effortlessly counter every tactic you try. No matter how you parade around him, calculating how to shake him down, you won't succeed, because he will be familiar with your game. Ultimately, he will watch as you smother yourself underwater, as this is the only way to dismantle your evil tactics in the natural realm. A changed man will struggle to remain in love with his devilish wife because he will realize they are unequally yoked as a couple. Be wary of losing your husband if you have not yet sought your transformation; transformation must go both ways.

Transformation shapes our lives until we leave this earth. We cannot escape the necessity of transformation. Change, whether for good or bad, is inevitable. What is wonderful, though, is when a man changes for the better and starts pouring love into his relationships with his family and friends. He discovers the right chords to play so that harmonious music will resound through his life and marriage, in synchrony with his wife's heart and soul. This incredible man pledges to stay disciplined, control his behavior, keep his word, and orchestrate peace in every situation. He understands the importance of handling every instance of chaos and disorder with grace.

Hold onto your patience during your husband's transformation. God is operating on him, and that procedure cannot be rushed. You must remain submissive to your husband while he is being pulled from one end to the other. Step into his shoes for a moment and think about what he is feeling: He knows something is going on with him – something is unraveling inside his soul, or perhaps peeling away from his skin – but he has no idea what! Can you imagine how disturbing that must be for him?

When God performs this operation, we must step back like nurses in the operation room and only come forth when we have been called to help the surgeon. At all other times, we should stand aside in compliance and respect. We must be prepared to see this journey through to the end, knowing we will be tested in areas we may have considered deal-breakers before we got married. Rushing God's operation will not bring you results any faster; instead, you may end up botching the procedure entirely and pushing your husband even further into the dark tunnel through which he is traveling. Have faith that God is working on His timeline, and know that any obstacles you face are only temporary.

If you are both embracing transformations together, you should celebrate your bond. It is so exciting to know your marriage is aligned and you are seeking stability and growth without interruption, making your way hand in hand toward Victory Street. Grip your husband's hand tightly, and watch him humbly align his goals in life with yours to secure an inheritance for his family. It is worth the wait!

Despite what others may say about your husband, hang in there if you see something special within him. His transformation is coming!

As I have stated before, transformation helps our relationships flourish. We all should move forward in life honoring every transformation that comes our way. Think about how many classrooms you passed through in grade school, year after year until you finally graduated from high school. Transformation comes in periodic stages just like that. When you first say "I do" to each other, you enter the kindergarten stage of marriage. As the years pass and you face each stage of transformation together, your hearts and souls will develop in tandem, and you will learn to adapt how you approach each other to deal with the issues coming from your hearts. It is going to be okay! That is all that you have to remember if you are willing to fight for your marriage.

Hopefully, you are now aware of the love and understanding needed from you to guide your husband as he transforms into that better man you hoped he would become. You must stay attuned to his temperament during this process. Most women enjoy the experience of receiving a makeover, whether externally or internally. Some women even find it comforting. But it is difficult for a man to embrace change, so you must hold his hand and soothe his fears. It will be difficult. It will be scary. But it will be the best effort you will ever expend. Helping him through his transformation doesn't require heavy studying, just patience, and support!

Here is the road map to guiding your husband through his transformation:

1. Overcome negative reactions with grace.
2. Keep your husband's compass pointed in the right direction by providing positive feedback.

3. Ignore his rage when he is in the operating room with God.

4. If you have not sought your transformation, clean your heart, and renew your mind. Otherwise, his discernment will be too much for you to handle.

5. Pray that he glides through the gates of transformation.

6. If he is not ready yet, pray, be still, and lead him toward the path of transformation.

Chapter 15

You Made It To Victory Street!

Throughout this book, I have expressed the importance of striving to reach Victory Street because reaching this milestone is the key to an everlasting marriage. Victory Street is what lies on the other side of all the hard times and persecutions that you have faced. Once you reach it, you will gain access to a spectrum of life that never expires. Reaching Victory Street is an honor, and accordingly, it bestows instant and never-ending happiness upon you and your husband. Here, you will discover the divine blueprint for your marriage that outlines God's directions for your lives. To arrive at Victory Street, both you and your husband must overcome the hardships in your path with patience and gratitude.

If you have understood your respective roles in your marriage as a designated spiritual leader and loyal wife, you will witness the difference you can make, and you will experience unlimited joy. Couples who reach this point in their marriage have successfully navigated the dark tunnel; a victorious, harmonious life awaits them that is replete with vibrant rainbows and rejuvenating fresh air. This is a paradise that cannot be denied by those who see you – and people *will* see you. When you reach this point in your marriage, other couples will watch you as if your marriage is a movie, wondering how to avoid pitfalls so they can rejoice in victory with you. When you are living in a victorious marriage, the movie only ends when God calls you to your final home to reclaim the mansion He built for you two. If you have been dedicated to your marriage vows and covenant with God, it is the truth that you will remain hand in hand 'til death do you part!

The path to Victory Street is not straightforward. Pain and agony can derail you and stall compromise, but you must remain focused to find your way. Even if you start over in a new marriage, you will continue to learn from your previous tribulations, and you will mature in the face of adversity. The road you travel is often dotted with potholes and ditches that you have to avoid or carefully rollover to prevent damage to your relationships. Remember that adversity and setbacks are a part of growth, especially in your marriage. All you need is for one person in your marriage to stay focused on reaching Victory Street! Keep your feet planted on solid ground, and keep your eye on the prize.

Listen, you will not achieve victory by succumbing to every setback and allowing negative emotions and the opinions of others to take over. When you are fighting for your marriage, you will often need to take "the road less traveled." No one else knows what God has in store for you and your relationship, so you must be careful what you allow to infiltrate your marriage and send you down a detour from what has been divinely designed for you. It takes a mature couple to stay the course, but if you endure, you will have harmony – *that's* the victory!

Of course, endurance does not come overnight. How many people envision their marriage making it to the golden years but end up falling short because they succumb to obstacles and roadblocks? And how many men believe Cinderella will come running to their doors with her glass slippers, requiring no effort on their part to keep the vision of marriage alive?

If you realize you have fallen out of love with your spouse and pursue a divorce, the shortcuts you have been taking all these years will lead you to a dead end. In seeking remarriage, you are consciously deciding to start over entirely and reopen your wounds in the process of making room for your new spouse to join you on your journey. You will have to return to square one to learn your new spouse's ups and downs!

In many ways, you will marry your spouse multiple times through each level of growth and deeper commitment you encounter in your marriage. At twenty years old, you learn to overcome challenges together; at fifty years old, you become each other's strength and support. At seventy years old, you will be cruising down Victory Street without a care in the world!

Victory Street is the key to eternal peace and happiness in your marriage, but it is the most difficult key to obtain. This key cannot be duplicated or copied. It has been locked inside the safety box of your and your partner's hearts, and it can only be retrieved when you realize there is no right or wrong in your marriage, no matter the situation. Love covers all, but remember: You must love yourself first.

You may spend years fighting for your marriage, working diligently to find the code to that safety box so you can finally gain entry to the golden years of marriage. However, holding that key in your hands will make your efforts worth it! When you and your husband fight to stay together, you will secure the livelihoods of the family and witness endorsement of your faith from all of your loved ones. Your parents and siblings will hold you as a standard for their marriages, and your children will carry on the legacy of your vision into their future relationships. That alone will transport you and your family to Victory Street! By displaying the struggles and rewards of marriage, you are knitting a beautiful cloth of love to pass to your children, and they will pass that cloth down in turn for generations to come. Your bond with your husband will be timeless and unbreakable.

The rewards of taking shortcuts in the journey of marriage are plentiful, but they are not easy to obtain. Only trust will get you to Victory Street. Trust means continuing to walk down the path without worrying about what your spouse is doing! Trust means knowing your spouse will be beside you without having to look. Trust stands hand in hand with peace in the marriage. When you trust each other, you do not fantasize or daydream about other outcomes. Everything that you and your husband have discussed effortlessly becomes reality. Blessings cover you, allowing you to overcome disturbances without any struggle.

Yes, you can lose your way if you let go of your faith, even after you've reached Victory Street. So never forget that faith is what guides you. Victory

Street is a special place! There is peace on every corner and no dead ends insight. When you travel down Victory Street, you travel higher and higher in life. Countless doors of opportunity and wealth are open to you. Your whole perspective of life will be changed because you will realize there is a reason for everything you fought through.

I know you may not agree with me. You may say that you didn't find The One until your second or third marriage, and now everything is on the right track. That may be true if you genuinely have no more room to grow (whether emotionally, spiritually, or even financially) and have determined exactly who completes you. However, don't confuse a high standard of living and joint households and bank accounts with Victory Street. You may have been able to reach Victory Street with your previous partners as well. And I am sure plenty of remarried couples are completely unaware of how essential their past relationships were to their current success.

Victory Street is the end goal of marriage. You will hear myriad opinions from people in your life about your decision to stay in your marriage; your girlfriends may even tell you to leave your spouse and find another relationship. However, people who suggest this do not understand that you will go through changes regardless of who your spouse is! Holding onto your vision is important in the face of these criticisms. Clutch the image of Victory Street close to your heart, and know that you can overcome any pain, hurt, and disappointment to reach that paradise.

The peace and harmony that you will achieve on Victory Street form the glue that pulls the pieces of your love into a priceless ceramic masterpiece! Be thankful for every obstacle that challenges you to grow, every cliff that encourages you to take a leap of faith, and, most of all, every hard landing that increases your endurance for the next trial, as these are the experiences that teach you to fulfill your covenant with God and reach Victory Street. Understand that *no one's* relationship is perfect from the start; it becomes more perfect in grace when you don't give up!

If you still doubt the merits of fighting to stay together, ask your parents or your grandparents how they stayed together for so long. I guarantee they will agree with me completely on the importance of displaying gratitude and fortitude. On Victory Street, gratitude will replace your fears and worries and reward you with good health and wealth. But first, your love for each other must be solid, with God as your rock! As stated in Psalms 119:33, "Teach me, O Lord, the way of thy statutes; and I shall keep it unto the end." The keyword here is "keep": You will not reach Victory Street unless you take God's teachings to heart! Ride the wave of disagreements and hardships in a God-fearing way, and keep in mind that you have been influenced positively so you can positively help others as well.

When your resolve wavers, remember God's promise to always lead us to victory, regardless of what we are facing. Place your trust in God, know you will overcome your struggles, and stand up for what you know is right! This is the mindset you must achieve – a mindset of steady determination – to continue fighting for your goals and to take your marriage all the way to Victory Street. God promises to lavish His favor upon married couples who agree to fight for their relationships. When both of you decide to stand your ground, the good love begins.

Every problem solves itself with time, so let go of the drama and give everything to God! Remember that you travel on the promises of God, and His promises will give you new life. Aim to embody peace and grace in all you do, aim to accept change for the best, and most importantly of all, aim to push on to Victory Street!

It's time to complete my journey of sharing my tips for surviving marriage. Here is the final road map for remaining on Victory Street:

1. Celebrate yourself.
2. Focus on maintaining harmony.
3. Never take the long road; always take the shortcuts.
4. Internalize a peaceful approach to conflict and run for your goals.
5. Sit back and watch God pave your way to Victory Street.

Made in the USA
Columbia, SC
18 September 2024